Medieval Armour

Medieval Armour

Martin J. Dougherty

amber
BOOKS

Amber Books Ltd
United House
North Road
London N7 9DP
United Kingdom

www.amberbooks.co.uk
Facebook: amberbooks
YouTube: amberbooksltd
Instagram: amberbooksltd
X(Twitter): @amberbooks

ISBN: 978-1-83886-663-1

Editorial, design and picture research: Amber Books Ltd

Printed and bound in China

About the Author:
Martin J. Dougherty is the author of *Samurai Armour*, *Greek Myths* and *Celts*, among many other titles. A former defence consultant, he has written numerous books on history and military history, including *Vikings: A History of the Norse People*, *The Wars of the Roses*, *King Arthur and the Knights of the Round Table* and *Kings & Queens of the Medieval World.*

Contents

Introduction

THE MEDIEVAL PERIOD is generally considered to span roughly from 500 to 1500CE, falling between the Roman era and the Renaissance. This was a time of great change, much of it resulting from territorial wars and succession disputes. Militarily, the focus shifted from infantry forces to cavalry as the main striking arm, and since most conflicts were of relatively small scale, the prowess of individual warriors could be a decisive factor.

Opposite: This 16th-century German illustration shows an idealized scene of two knights entering a tournament, both men and their horses fully armoured, with jousting lances poised for combat.

At the beginning of the medieval period, warriors typically wore chain mail for protection, whereas by its end they had donned full-body suits of articulated plate. Weapons evolved alongside armour, producing specialist anti-armour arms, such as the war pick and the estoc – a thrusting sword with a triangular cross-section blade designed to penetrate mail or the gaps in plate armour.

The Early Medieval period began with large-scale population movements caused by incursions from the east. Successive waves of invaders, notably the Huns, pushed tribes westwards and caused severe disruption. At around the same time, Germanic tribes were migrating across the North Sea into the British Isles and coming into conflict with the post-Roman population there.

After 800CE, the era of mass migrations came to an end, marking the dawn of the Viking Age in which Scandinavian warriors raided all over Europe and even into the Mediterranean. Raids expanded into conquest, making the Norsemen part of the European political landscape. Other Norse adventurers went east, integrating into the Slavic cultures of Novgorod and Kiev as a ruling warrior–noble class.

Each upheaval contributed to a new order emerging in Europe. By 1000CE, the mounted warrior was king of the battlefield, having relegated infantry to a supporting role. This was the era of William the Conqueror, a Norman duke who took advantage of a succession dispute in England to make himself king.

If the Early Medieval period was characterized by the establishment of new states, European history from 1000CE onwards was dominated by territorial and succession disputes between them, and by religious conflict. A series of crusades in the Holy Land and elsewhere, starting in 1095, mobilized European military forces, drained treasuries and occasionally triggered additional conflicts. The death of a relatively young monarch or a setback in a crusade might result in a rebellion or succession dispute unrelated to the event itself.

At the same time, technology was advancing. Mail armour was reinforced with plate and eventually replaced entirely by it. The classic image of the 'knight in shining armour' only appeared in the late medieval period, at a time when European kingdoms were relatively well established. The weapons and equipment of a 15th-century knight would likely have astonished – or perhaps dismayed – a warrior from the post-Roman era.

It might seem that firearms swept the armoured knight off the battlefield, but this was not so. Armour strong enough to withstand contemporary firearms was still in use, and the main threat to a knight remained another heavily armoured warrior wielding weapons designed to penetrate it. Massive social upheaval, largely caused by the devastating Black Death, brought with it changes in how wars were waged. However, the armoured horseman continued to be a force to be reckoned with into the Renaissance period. His armour changed over time, but the cavalry during the Wars of Religion in the 16th and 17th centuries still wore half-plate. Even as late as the Napoleonic era, French heavy cavalry were equipped with a metal breastplate and helmet for protection.

The last hurrah of the armoured horseman came during World War I, nearly five centuries after the medieval period had ended. By then, armour had changed little, making it reasonable to say that personal armour design reached its peak during the late medieval period.

This illustration from a 14th-century prayer book depicts the victory of Walter von Klingen in a formal tournament, and the admiration of watching noblewomen.

CHAPTER 1

Historical Context

The arms race between the destructive power of weapons and the creation of suitable protection began in the ancient past. The natural weapons of a human are rather feeble compared to those of other predators, and while fists and perhaps biting would suffice to harm another person, it was necessary to turn the human talent for toolmaking to the creation of weapons capable of bringing down large and dangerous animals. These weapons could also be turned against fellow humans if some dispute arose.

Prehistoric Times

Clothing provided protection against the elements and minor natural hazards. Tough foot coverings prevented damage to the feet from sharp stones, while clothed limbs were less likely to be scratched by thorns. There was a logical progression towards creating improved versions of these clothes in the hope of mitigating the damage caused by an enemy's weapon.

A Bronze Age stele found in Spain depicts a warrior equipped in a manner that remained largely unchanged for centuries. He is armed with a spear as a main weapon, carries a sword as a sidearm, and is protected by a shield and helmet.

In these ancient times the materials for weapon and armour making were only those that could be obtained in their raw state. Animal hides and sinew, bone, and perhaps bark or some similar material could be used to create primitive forms of armour that might offer some protection against the weapons of the day – spears, clubs, javelins and arrows.

Metal offered far more options, but was difficult to obtain and work with. Soft metals like copper and gold could be found in their native state, and removed from the surrounding rock by pounding with a stone. Copper could be worked cold by bashing it with something hard, creating sharp edges and useful pieces. However, the ability to shape copper in this way meant that it would soon lose its edge or become deformed.

Metal was sufficiently useful that experimentation continued, and over time smiths learned how to heat metals and blend them together. Bronze, an alloy of copper, tin and sometimes other materials, was one of the most significant discoveries in human history. While a finely made stone tool could be as effective as a bronze one, bronze items could be made more quickly and to suit a greater diversity of applications.

Early Metal Armour

From around 3000BCE, metal equipment revolutionized warfare. Ancient Sumerian soldiers were equipped with bronze or copper helmets and protected by thick cloaks strengthened by metal discs

Mesopotamian warriors circa 2500BCE. Fighting in close order with spears and protected by helmets and cloaks studded with metal discs, these early infantry enjoyed huge advantages over their less organized and poorly equipped enemies.

Warriors of Egypt's New Kingdom era (c. 1390–1352 BCE) wore armour made of small scales like this one, either fixed together by cords or sewn onto a suitable backing.

sewn onto them. This personal armour made the weapons they faced – typically war clubs used by less organized tribal societies in the region – largely ineffective.

These Sumerian fighters were armed with metal-tipped spears that were more effective than the weaponry of their opponents, and they fought in close order as soldiers rather than hunters-turned-warriors.

A bronze cuirass (breastplate) of the Hallstatt-era Celtic culture of the upper Danube region offered strong protection for the vital organs, although at the cost of some freedom of movement. This example dates from around 1200BCE.

A Babylonian charioteer and archer, both protected by scale armour, could bring firepower to bear on the enemy then retire quickly if the response was too intense.

Armour scales from Egypt, c.589–570BCE. Scales of varying sizes were used to allow both mobility and coverage for the human body's irregularly shaped parts.

A bronze Corinthian helmet from the 7th–6th century BCE, *designed to deflect spear thrusts or downward sword blows. Those who could afford such helmets were placed at the front lines, earning honour and social status – assuming they survived the battle.*

Superior military equipment enabled more effective tactics, which in turn allowed the city-states of ancient Mesopotamia to dominate the region. Civilized states pushed less organized tribal groups out of the land they wanted, and once it was secured the other trappings of civilization could flourish.

Similar events occurred elsewhere across Europe and Asia, with local preferences for weapons and fighting styles driving the development of armour to protect against them. The ancient Greek city-states settled their differences with massed spear-armed formations, and those who could afford it obtained protection against a spearpoint. The preference was for a thick bronze breastplate and a helmet providing almost full-face protection, as these were the areas most likely to be struck. Even before ironworking became prevalent, the basic forms of armour and weapons were in place.

Influences on Armour Design

Weapons cause injury in three main ways. Impaling weapons – which range from spears through arrows to bullets – rely on force concentrated at a single point to pierce the body. They are most likely to strike the torso, or perhaps the head in the case of a spear thrust, and can cause fatal injury through even a small penetration if a vital organ is pierced.

Cutting weapons also concentrate force behind a small area, but this is an edge rather than a point and the injury mechanics are different. A sufficiently heavy sharp implement can chop straight

Above: A 4th-century BCE Greek cuirass, often used alongside greaves and a helmet. Some Greek warriors are said to have gone into battle without any other clothing.

Opposite: Bronze greaves dating from the 5th century BCE. The lower legs are relatively easy to protect with single-piece armour, unlike many other areas of the body.

through flesh and bone, but most cutting weapons rely on a slicing action. A cutting weapon is less likely to cause a fatal injury but can slice through muscle and sinews to render a body part unusable and can also cause severe bleeding.

Blunt weapons rely on the impact of a heavy object to cause physical trauma. They are more likely to break bones than cutting weapons. The effects of this can vary: a broken arm is out of action, for example, making the fighter highly vulnerable, whereas a blunt force blow to the head might not penetrate a helmet but could still fracture the skull or at least disorientate the target.

The sorts of weapons favoured by potential enemies was a major influence on the design and construction of armour. Since cutting and blunt weapons rely on moving in an arc to cause damage, they are more likely to land on the arms or head than the torso. By contrast, spears and arrows tend to strike the body's centre of mass, and are therefore more likely to cause fatal injury. Armour had to balance sufficient protection with weight and cost, sometimes leaving less critical areas scantily defended in order to be able to shield against a fatal strike elsewhere.

The Iron Age

Ironworking became widespread in Europe around 1500BCE. Although the skill existed earlier, the difficulty of heating iron to workable temperatures made iron objects rare. In fact, a well-crafted bronze weapon or helmet could be as effective as early iron equivalents.

A Celtic shield from the La Tène era, around 500BCE. Warriors equipped with shields like this were key opponents of the emerging Roman Republic, shaping its choice of weapons and armour.

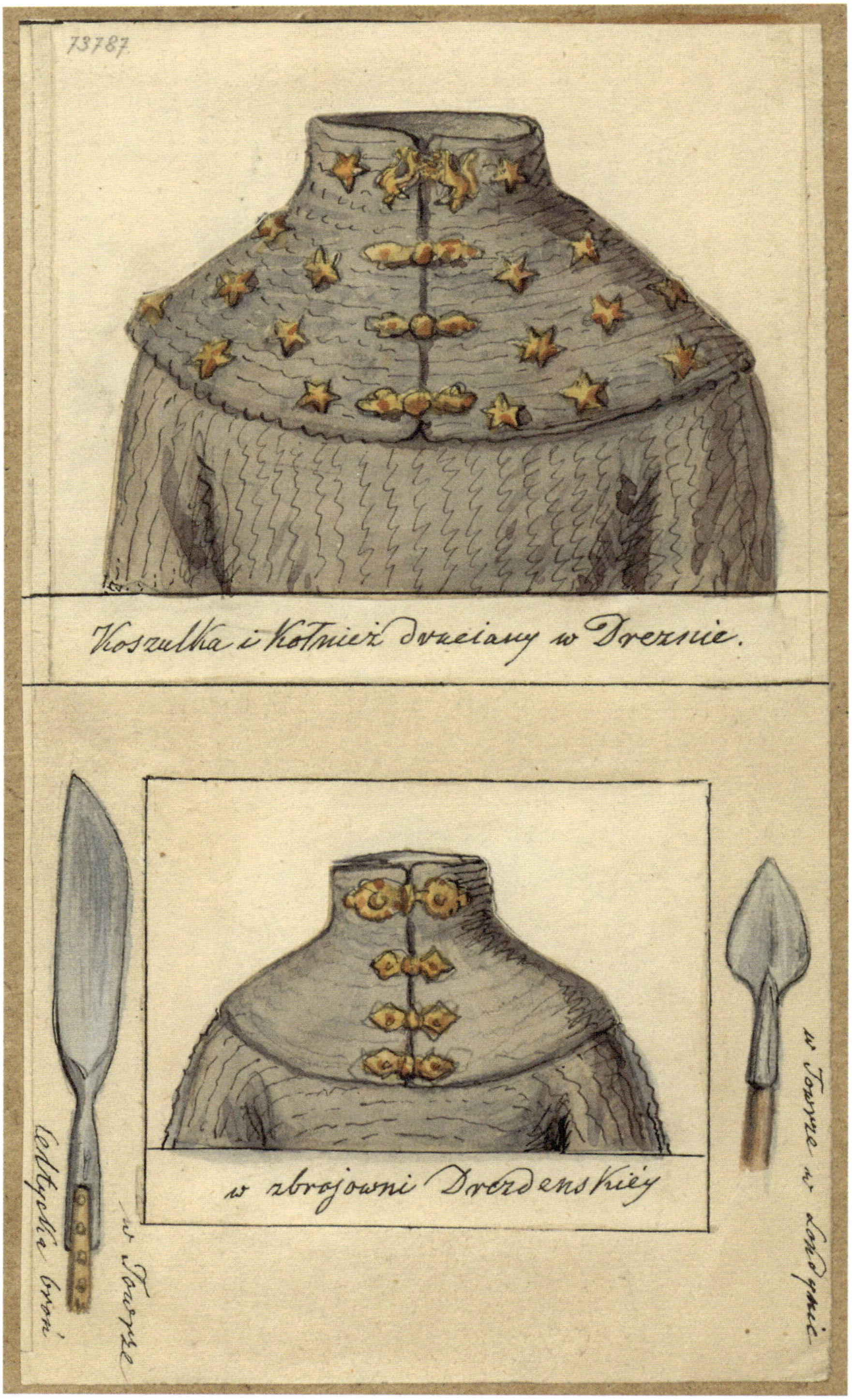

Protecting the neck and shoulders has always been important yet challenging, since mobility must not be impaired. One solution was to create a separate piece that could be draped over the shoulders, as shown here in this drawing based on a sixth century Celtic example.

A carving from Syria's Iron Age, c.1200–900BCE, depicts an armoured warrior on horseback, equipped with helmet and shield. At this time, stirrups had not yet been invented.

THE ROMAN ARMOUR REVOLUTION

In the early days of the Roman Republic, citizens serving in the military were expected to provide their own arms and equipment. Those who could afford to outfit themselves to a high standard were grouped together, with more lightly armed troops supporting them. This system functioned for decades, but a growing demand for more troops forced major reforms. Afterwards, arms and armour were standardized and supplied by the state. Such were the resources of the Roman Republic, and later empire, that ordinary soldiers could be armoured in metal.

Roman armour was designed to suit the weapons of likely opponents. 'Bbarbarian' enemies often fought with spears and long-bladed cutting swords. While the Roman soldier's shield offered good protection, spear thrusts and downward blows aimed at the head and shoulders remained dangerous. Helmets and shoulder armour were therefore shaped to deflect such attacks.

Conflict in Dacia and Thracia exposed Roman soldiers to long-bladed cutting weapons, such as the falx and the rhomphaia, which could reach under shields to slash the legs. These were countered by the use of greaves to protect the lower legs. This arrangement of armour helped Rome maintain its dominance over much of Europe for centuries and continued to influence armour design even after the empire's fall.

A pair of 4th-century BCE bone carvings found in Italy depict warriors equipped in a style more typically associated with ancient Greece, reflecting the Greek influence on Roman arms and armour.

Armour develops in response to threat. When Roman troops faced enemies wielding long-hafted weapons capable of striking beneath their shields, they responded by adding protective elements that previously had not been considered necessary.

It is widely accepted that the classic Roman shield, or scutum, was curved rather than flat. This increased its defensive value by deflecting blows and missiles.

This funerary stele commemorates Titus Calidius Severus, a centurion of Legio XV Apollinaris. It shows typical centurion equipment, including lorica squamata *(scale armour) and a helmet with a transverse crest.*

Once forging techniques were sufficiently advanced, iron gradually began to supplant bronze as the standard metal component in high-quality armour.

Warriors of this era relied heavily on shields to defend against hand weapons and projectiles. While shields sizes varied, they were generally large enough to limit the available targets to the head and lower legs, at least most of the time. Unlike passive armour, shields were used actively to impede an enemy and could also serve as a weapon. A warrior with a shield and head protection was nearly as well-protected as one wearing full torso armour – but only nearly. Those who could afford it still obtained the best armour they could, regardless of their skill with a shield.

Chain mail, created by interlinking rings of metal, was developed during this period. Its development is typically attributed to the Celtic tribes of the Upper Danube Valley. As with most military innovations, those that encountered warriors armoured in mail sought to acquire it for themselves. Time-consuming and labour-intensive to produce, chain mail was expensive and limited only to the upper echelons of society.

The Mounted Warrior

Horses have been used in warfare since ancient times. Initially their role was to pull chariots, as the horses of the time were too small to carry a fully equipped warrior. Riders served usefully as messengers and scouts, but true mounted combat did not emerged until around 1200BCE. Even then, mounted warriors were mainly lightly armed skirmishers or horse archers.

As larger and more sturdy horses were bred, recognizable cavalry began to emerge. Some militaries used a mix of cavalry and chariots, gaining the advantages of both, but in the Roman era the chariot was considered archaic and unsuited to warfare in most regions. The British Isles was a notable exception, but in most places the military system began to fall into a pattern of armoured cavalry, lighter cavalry, foot soldiers and missile troops. Of these, the armoured cavalry had the highest status and foot soldiers typically the lowest.

This is a huge generalization, of course, but social and military status were generally intertwined. Those who could afford a horse, armour and weapons belonged to the upper ranks of society. They received formal martial training and were much more likely to survive a battle than foot soldiers thanks to their skills, mobility and personal protection. Some societies valued their foot soldiers as professionals, while others simply thrust a mass of ill-equipped peasants on the battlefield to make up numbers.

Across much of Europe, terms associated with nobility are derived from horse ownership. The German title 'Ritter' literally means 'rider', while the concept of chivalry, the code of honour supposedly followed by the nobility, comes from the Italian *cavalleria* – the same origin as the word 'cavalry', referring to mounted soldiers.

The social order varied somewhat from one region to another, but essentially the uppermost was a military elite, with a middle class composed of various professionals beneath them, all above a peasantry consisting of labourers and farmers. This was not a simple system; there were ranks and distinctions within each group, but most importantly there was a sharp divide between the nobility and everyone else.

The titles used by high nobility originated from various sources and were often highly specific to a region or role. In what later became England, for example, the title duke (derived from the Latin 'Dux', meaning a senior Roman military-political leader) was reserved for

This illustration shows a Roman auxiliary cavalryman, circa the first century BCE. He carries a long spear and shield, and wears lorica squamata, *a form of scale armour favoured by Roman cavalrymen because of its flexibility.*

Relief depicting Marcus Curtius throwing himself into a chasm, from the Lacus Curtius in the Roman Forum, Rome (fourth century BCE). He wears the trademark pteruges*, the reinforced leather skirt used to protect Roman soldiers. Hanging from the waist, this style of armour allowed flexibility and movement.*

A relief dating to around 30BCE shows a cavalry melee, with riders on both sides protected by shields, body armour and helmets. Dealing a decisive blow in such chaotic circumstances often depended on seizing a brief opportunity, such as when an opponent was distracted by another attacker.

An Anglo-Saxon relief dating from the 8th–9th century CE *depicts armoured warriors on horseback together with St Daniel and lions.*

members of the royal family. When the eldest son inherited the crown, his brothers would receive a duchy, ensuring they were not left impoverished and reducing the risk of rebellion. In other areas, some titles reflected the stated duties of a role, such as 'Markgraf', a Germanic title specific to a noble tasked with securing a *mark* (or march), which was a border region.

Parthian cataphract (1st century BCE). Parthian cataphracts wore full-body lamellar armour, with helmets, limb guards, and armoured horses, designed for powerful, close-range shock combat.

The Feudal System

After the fall of the Roman Empire, a feudal system emerged, theoretically structured around responsibilities owed to those above and below in the social hierarchy. In practice, obligations to one's superiors outweighed duties to the peasantry. The system relied on oaths of fealty, an ancient European practice, in which each individual pledged loyalty to a person one level higher in the hierarchy.

Land was owned by the nobility, who governed over the common people living on it. The court of a noble functioned as a law court, with justice dispensed at the noble's discretion. Nobles directed the commoners when there were large-scale tasks to undertake, settled disputes, suppressed banditry and provided the stability necessary for society to function. Naturally, in a system granting such absolute power, much depended on the character of the individual noble.

At the lowest level of nobility were those generally known as knights, although various other terms were also used. During the early medieval period, entry to this class was relatively informal and primarily depended on owning the proper equipment.

Over time, formal requirements and ceremonies for knighthood were established. Since horses and gear were expensive to acquire and maintain, a knight needed an income. This was usually drawn from taxes levied on the commoners living within his domain.

Some knights ranked above others and had the authority to command them in battle; these were known as bannerets and could

An 8th century carved stone relief from Germany, the Rider Stone of Hornhausen depicts an elite Frankish warrior, part of the emerging aristocratic warrior class of the early medieval period. He is armed with a lance, sword and round shield.

display a banner for identification. Knights and bannerets formed the lowest level of the nobility. Above them were the peers, collectively known as lords, each of whom owed loyalty to a superior, extending all the way up to the monarch.

Feudal warfare relied on the right of high-ranking nobles to demand military service from their subordinates. A senior noble would summon his vassals to form an army, each of whom was required to supply a number of knights and soldiers. Although the primary fighting arm of the Middle Ages was the armoured cavalryman, these represented only a small percentage of the overall army. Numbers could be made up by conscripting the peasantry, who were bound to serve when called upon. Although some members of these local militias possessed suitable weapons and a degree of training, they were generally poorly equipped and lacked the discipline and effectiveness of professional soldiers.

Above: Initially, owning a horse, sword and armour was sufficient to gain entry to the knightly class. Gradually, however, knights' lives became regulated by a formal code of courtesies and the obligation to pay homage to their lord.

A Swiss knight of the 1400s, shown with his page and squire. Serving a knight provided on-the-job training and a structured path into the knightly class.

A depiction of the Siege of Orleans in 1429, set in the Late Medieval period when armour-making had reached its peak in Europe. Although heavy, well-fitted articulated plate armour allowed full mobility and did not hinder physical activity.

Far more useful were the professional fighting men who straddled the line between nobility and commoners. While others went into the clergy or became important through their status as master craftsmen, these people equipped themselves for war and obtained training. Some served on foot as professional soldiers, some as light cavalry, and those who could afford it equipped themselves in the manner of a knight and rode into battle alongside them.

There is an enduring impression that warfare in this era was amateurish, and to some extent it was. Its focus differed greatly from that of Roman times and later eras when states fielded huge armies. Combat was often personal with leadership by example, but more importantly warfare revolved around large-scale raids and the capture or defence of castles and other strongholds. Successful military commanders needed to master both siege warfare and the political ramifications of their actions. Strategically, they were as skilled as leaders of other periods. Tactics, however, were a different matter. Given that the era's military strength rested with men who could elevate their position or gain wealth through bravery on the battlefield – and who were highly conscious of their standing among their peers – discipline in the field was often limited. Battlefield manoeuvres were necessarily simple, yet still might be derailed. A competent commander aimed to bring maximum force to bear where it mattered most, but his plans could be undone by a headstrong subordinate keen to claim the honour of engaging the enemy first.

Opposite: The Battle of Evesham, fought in 1265 during the High Medieval period, occurred at a time when mail (chain armour) was the main form of personal protection. Warriors typically wore a helm and carried a shield designed for use on horseback.

After the Fall of Rome

The fall of the Roman Empire is often dated at 476CE, but the empire did not collapse in an instant. It gradually weakened and lost control over territories, some of which were deliberately abandoned to reinforce more important possessions. By the final days of the empire, the iconic Roman legionary in his distinctive armour had been replaced by warriors equipped and fighting in the style of their native people, although influences remained.

Europe at this time was very troubled. Successive waves of invaders from the east, notably the Huns, forced tribal confederations to move west in search of safer lands. This period is known as the Volkswanderung, or Migration Period (476–800CE). Conflict between the displaced tribes and those whose lands they wanted to pass through or take for themselves was inevitable.

The term 'Dark Ages' is often used to describe the period after the fall of the Roman Empire, often encouraging images of barbaric chaos and destruction. Yet although violence was widespread, this era also saw the rise of new states. Cathedrals were built, along with other great projects that required stability and organization. The foundations of modern Europe can be said to have been laid during these centuries.

The period roughly spanning 500 to 1000CE is known as the Early Medieval period. It overlaps the Migration Period, with a gradual trend towards stability and the establishment of organized kingdoms. In what is now France the dominant power was the Franks, who were originally a Germanic group who had migrated west. The Frankish Kingdom

The Huns entering Rome, led by Attila, *by Ulpiano Checa (1887). The Huns waged war in a starkly different way to the failing Roman empire, relying on speed and surprise to overwhelm more heavily armoured opponents.*

was ruled by the Merovingian and later Carolingian dynasties, whose members included Charles Martel and Charlemagne.

Early in the period, England was divided into several kingdoms that fought among themselves and against Germanic invaders such as the Angles and Saxons. By 700CE England was divided into seven Anglo-Saxon kingdoms, with the Britons largely pushed west into Wales. The arrival of Norse raiders after 793CE was initially little more than a nuisance, but it marked the beginning of the 'Viking Age', a period that reshaped Europe.

Norse raids grew in size and strength, and within a few decades the raiding parties had become armies conquering large areas. The eastern

The Lindisfarne Stone depicts seven Norse warriors taking part in the first Viking raids in 793CE. Within a few decades, small-scale raiding gave way to large campaigns of conquest.

half of England fell under the control of Norse kingdoms, while a large Norse contingent had settled in northern France. These mixed Frankish and Norse cultures gave rise to the Kingdom of Normandy.

High Medieval Period

The Normans were a huge influence on European history. Their invasion of the British Isles, beginning in 1066, resulted in the defeat of the Anglo-Saxon and Norse kingdoms and the creation of a recognizable Kingdom of England. Norman adventurers carved out kingdoms elsewhere, notably in Sicily. A separate German Kingdom arose, encompassing what had been the eastern part of the Carolingian Empire, and other states emerged that still exist in some form today.

Territorial ambition and succession disputes fuelled conflicts throughout the era, with religious wars increasing in scale. At this time,

Charles Martel led the Frankish resistance to the Saracen invasion of Europe in the 8th century. This manuscript illustration from Les grandes chroniques de France *reflects the norms of the 15th century, with plate armour and heraldic symbols on display.*

The First Crusade (1096–99) distracted the kingdoms of Europe from fighting one another, pitting them against Muslim forces for control of the Holy Land. Godfrey, Count of Bouillon, is depicted here leading the Christian charge.

the Byzantine Empire still survived as a remnant of the Eastern Roman Empire, although it was under heavy pressure. The First Crusade, launched in 1095, was aimed at relieving Byzantium and returning the Holy Land to Christian control. It was followed by several more crusades in the Holy Land and elsewhere, including crusades against heretics within Europe.

The crusades brought European knights into conflict with others from vastly different cultures, prompting innovations in armour design. Protection that had been effective against the swords and lances of similarly equipped warriors was often ineffective against the arrows of highly mobile horse archers, who could strike from beyond the reach of a knight's charge.

In Iberia, the Reconquista, the Christian reconquest of the peninsula from Muslim rule, was ongoing. Iberia had been invaded by the Umayyad Caliphate in the early 700s, and although the invasion was turned back by the Franks, most of Iberia remained under Muslim control. By the start of the High Medieval period in the 11th century, some areas had been regained and Christian kingdoms established. Notable among these were Navarre, Leon, Aragon and Castile. The Spanish kingdoms grew in power and gradually expelled the Moors, although it was not until 1492 that the Reconquista was declared complete.

In the mid-1100s, civil war wracked England in a conflict so bitter it became known as the Anarchy. After this succession dispute was over, the power of the English throne grew until the kings of England also controlled much of France. Known as the Angevin Empire, this arrangement was complex as the lands in France were legally part of the Kingdom of France, and were held under a subordinate title that theoretically meant an English king had to show allegiance to the French monarch. This situation inevitably led to conflict, and the wars with France became intertwined with internal politics in England. The First Barons' War, beginning in 1215, saw English nobles rebel against King John of England.

At the same time, Europe faced a grave threat from the Mongol Empire, founded in 1206 by Genghis Khan. The Mongols conquered the fragmented principalities of Russia and pushed into Eastern Europe where their mobile fighting style came up against

THE ANGEVIN EMPIRE

The Angevin Empire emerged out of the Anarchy, a bitter power struggle resulting from the death of Henry I of England in 1135. Henry named his daughter Matilda, widow of the Holy Roman Emperor, as his successor. The English lords instead installed her cousin, Stephen of Blois, as king. Years of bloody fighting left Stephen on the throne but under conditions that ensured Henry II, son of Empress Matilda, became his heir.

Henry II inherited lands in Normandy from his mother and after marrying Eleanor of Aquitaine in 1152 became Duke of Aquitaine. In 1154 he inherited the crown of England, after which he conquered further lands to create a powerful empire. This did not sit well with the King of France, who technically could demand obeisance from Henry II as Duke of Aquitaine, but was likely to get a war instead.

In 1189, Henry II died and his son Richard I came to the throne. Richard, often called 'the Lionheart', seems to have regarded England mainly as a source of revenue to fund his participation in the crusades, and spent little time there. He was killed in battle in 1199, after which his brother John of England succeeded him as king.

John's reign was so disastrous for England that no subsequent king would bear that name. Almost all the Angevin holdings in France were lost and there was even a brief French invasion of England. John's own barons also rebelled against him, and by the time of his death in 1216, the Angevin Empire was no more.

the armoured troops of European kingdoms. The longbow made its appearance at around this time, giving English forces a significant advantage over many of their opponents.

The Late Medieval Period

The Late Medieval period is generally considered to have lasted from 1300 to 1500CE. Technology continued to develop throughout this era, creating new challenges for weapon makers. Notable among these was the introduction of firearms in the early 1300s. At first these were highly ineffective, but over time they became such a threat that armour had

Genghis Khan leads Mongol warriors in combat. The Mongols preferred lamellar or scale armour, made from small scales or plates fixed to a backing, which did not impede horsemanship or archery.

to be tested to ensure it could stop a pistol ball, or it risked rejection by the purchaser.

The outbreak of the Hundred Years War in 1337 saw the kingdoms of England and France pitted against one another in a struggle that drew in forces from many other kingdoms. This conflict also affected relations between England and Scotland, the latter having entered into an alliance with France that could force the English to fight on two fronts.

Firearms and cannon were in their infancy at this time, and while guns were present at the decisive Battle of Crécy, they were greatly overshadowed by longbowmen protected by dismounted men-at-arms. The war finally came to an end in 1453, and was almost immediately

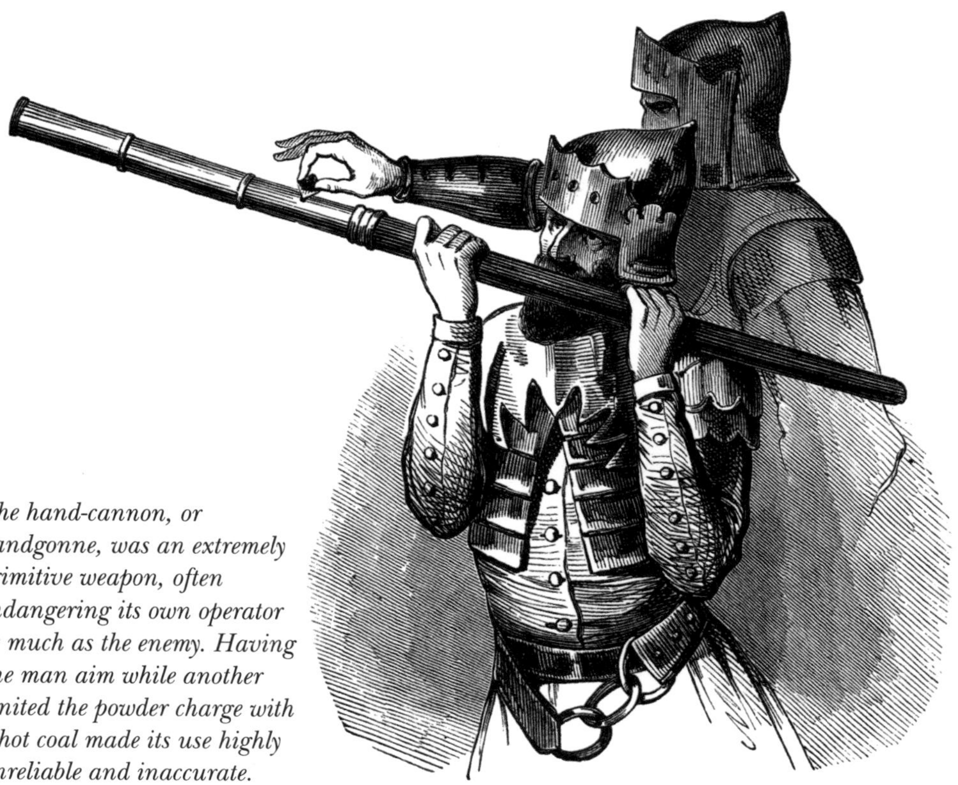

The hand-cannon, or handgonne, was an extremely primitive weapon, often endangering its own operator as much as the enemy. Having one man aim while another ignited the powder charge with a hot coal made its use highly unreliable and inaccurate.

THE HOLY ROMAN EMPIRE

In 768CE, Pepin the Short, King of the Franks, died and was succeeded by his son Charles. After conquering Lombardy and increasing the power of the Frankish Kingdom elsewhere, Charles was crowned Emperor of the Romans by Pope Leo III. He is better known to history as Charlemagne, first of the Carolingian dynasty.

At this time the term 'Romans' was commonly used to describe the civilized peoples of Europe, reflecting lingering admiration for the legacy of the Roman Empire. The label 'Holy Roman Empire' is often used today for convenience to refer to the vast array of German principalities united under a common crown, although the term was not originally in use.

The empire gained the monicker 'Holy' in 1157, during the reign of Frederick I Barbarossa, and existed in one form or another until dissolved by Emperor Napoleon of France in 1806. By that time it was little more than a notion, but during the medieval period the Holy Roman Empire was one of the great powers in Europe – at times even the greatest.

followed by a series of civil wars in England known collectively as the Wars of the Roses. These lasted until 1487, by which time most of Europe was beginning to experience the Renaissance. England lingered in the medieval period for longer than other realms, but ultimately embraced the enormous social changes sweeping the rest of the continent.

The battle of Crécy (1346) largely saw heavily armoured French noble cavalry face English longbowmen and dismounted men-at-arms. Valiant as the French knights were, they were also disorganized and impetuous, at one point forcing their way through their own crossbow-armoured units to engage the enemy more quickly.

A cavalryman's half-armour manufactured in Nuremberg, Germany, around 1610–20CE. It shows Eastern influences, including a helmet design inspired by Turkish military equipment.

Developments in Military Equipment

During the medieval period, armour design advanced considerably. In the post-Roman, Early Medieval period, chain mail was the primary heavy armour component. Solid plates might be used on body parts that were easy to armour, but at this time the coat of mail was standard. Gradually, however, articulated plates became prevalent, with mail as a backup to guard areas that were difficult to cover.

The development of articulated plate armour was clearly influenced by the *lorica segmentata*, the quintessential body armour of the Roman legionary. The techniques of creating it were not a Roman invention, however. Like the *lorica hamata* chain mail armour used by many Roman troops, the technique of articulating armour plates was developed elsewhere. It was not until the later medieval period that articulated armour achieved its classic form, creating a suit that could resist most weapons – even firearms – yet allowed a skilled user the freedom of movement required to fight with hand weapons.

Development continued into the Renaissance period. As late as the 1600s, armoured cavalry and some foot soldiers were wearing half-armour covering their torso and the upper parts of their limbs. The metal breastplate was still in use by some troops during the Napoleonic era.

Vestiges of medieval-style armour persisted into recent times in the form of a gorget worn by officers. Originally a throat protector, the gorget evolved into a pendant with minimal protective value, serving instead as a symbol of rank. Since only the most high-ranking individuals would have been able to afford such armour in the medieval period, it is perhaps fitting that a stylized version came to denote status and authority in later armies.

The popular image of the 'knight in shining armour' comes from the later medieval period, around 1575. By then, the art of making articulated plate armour had reached its height, alongside the fully developed traditions of heraldry and chivalry.

CHAPTER 2

Types of Armour

Armour can be constructed from a variety of materials and is usually composed of more than one combined together. It is broadly categorized as either rigid or flexible, each type with both advantages and disadvantages. The relative hardness or softness of armour can also be important. For example, hard armour such as a metal plate can deflect a weapon, reducing its force, whereas softer materials might allow the point or edge to penetrate. Conversely, a heavy blow against a hard piece of armour might buckle it or transmit force to the wearer, while a softer material would have absorbed more of the impact.

The most basic armour is clothing made from tough material. Leather or hide is commonly used, but thick cloth can also serve the purpose. By nature, this type of armour is soft and flexible. It is good at absorbing the energy of a blow and can be crafted to resist cutting by sharp edges. Cloth or leather armour offers limited protection against impaling attacks, such as arrows and spears, which strike squarely, but it can slow, deflect or partially trap a projectile, often preventing serious harm to the wearer.

Soft armour of this type can be reinforced by adding pieces of hard material. If these are small and separated by flexible gaps, they do not impede movement. The same principle applies when hard materials are placed on areas that do not need to flex, such as strips along the forearms or shoulder guards. While metal is the most common choice, wood is occasionally used. These materials may be attached to the outside of the main armour or sewn inside it to create a layered defence.

Armour Development

Chain mail offers a balance between hardness and flexibility. It can be shaped to run over joints and awkward parts of the body in a similar manner to cloth or hide armour, but is much more resistant against the points or edges of weapons. Mail was the mainstay of personal armour in the Early Medieval period and remained a useful component even after it was replaced by articulated plate.

Solid plates, usually made of metal, offer what is arguably the best level of protection when balanced against weight and bulk. Some body areas are relatively easy to protect in this way due to their shape and lack of movement, such as the upper torso or lower limbs. However, providing coverage to joints posed a problem for armour makers. Alternatives were chain mail or loosely attached armour pieces, which would hopefully be in the right place when a blow arrived.

Once the problem of creating fully articulated armour pieces was solved it became possible to protect knees, elbows and other awkwardly shaped body parts. Over time, the myth arose that plate armour was so

Turcopoles 'Sons of Turks' were local men recruited in the Holy Land by the Crusaders and converted to Christianity. Some fought mounted, often as horse archers, while others were equipped as light infantry. This man wears a basic armour of quilt and a simple helmet. His spear is backed up by the traditional scimitar and small round shield of his home region.

heavy that knights had to be winched onto their horses and could move only with difficulty and in a clumsy stagger. In reality, knights were able to perform gymnastic feats in their armour to demonstrate their prowess.

No armour can provide 100 per cent protection against every kind of attack. Instead, it improves the wearer's chances of surviving

TYPES OF HAUBERK

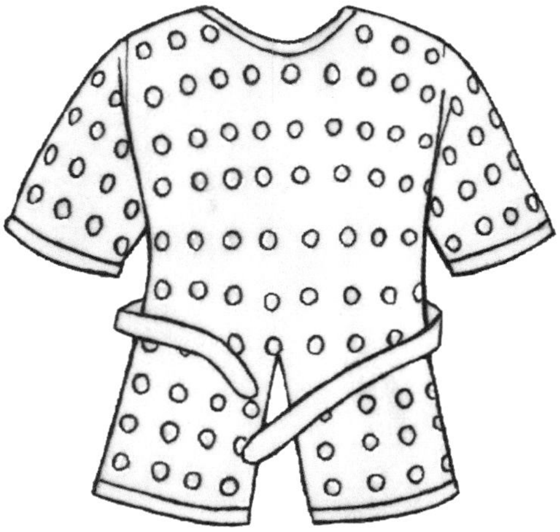

Studded Leather

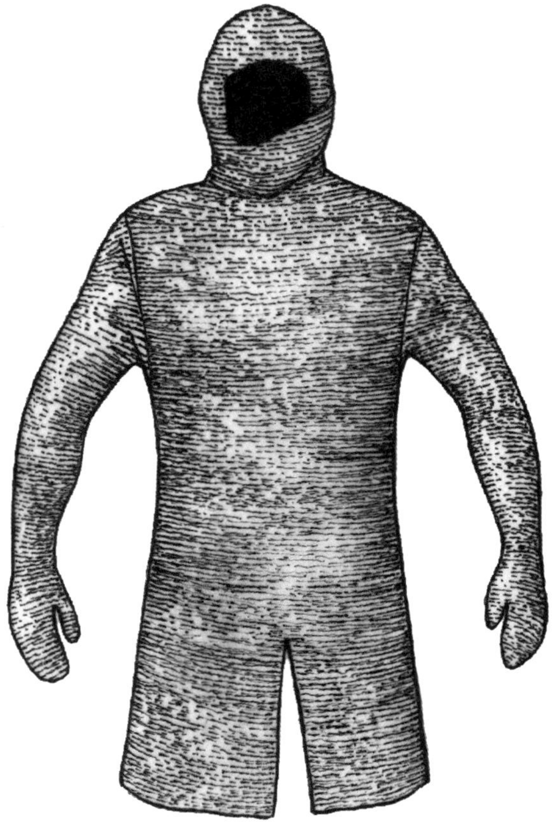

Chainmail

Scale Armour

A hauberk was a piece of armour that protected the torso and at least part of the limbs, with sleeves and a free-hanging skirt that covered the thighs. A hauberk was heavy, with most of the weight hanging on the wearer's shoulders, but it offered protection and reasonable mobility.
A hauberk consisted of a base garment of leather or thick cloth, to which additional protection was attached. Hauberks using metal studs or scales fixed to the leather base garment were easier to make than chainmail, which gave better protection but took a long time, and a great deal of skill, to produce.

KNIGHT'S CLOTHING (13TH CENTURY)

The primary protection of a knight in this period was provided by his hauberk of mail. This could be augmented by additional garments worn over or under it. The names of these garments have at times been used interchangeably, and others have at times been applied, but most commonly the word gambeson applies to a quilted jerkin that could be worn under the hauberk to give extra padding. A similar garment worn over armour was named an aketon. These two layers of padding, with the hauberk in between, offered excellent, if bulky, protection.

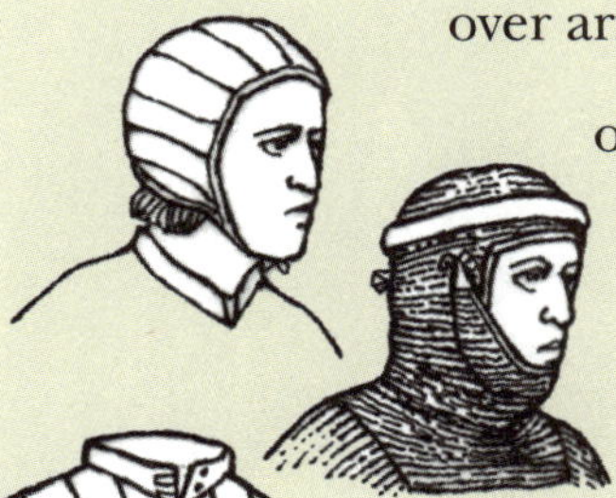

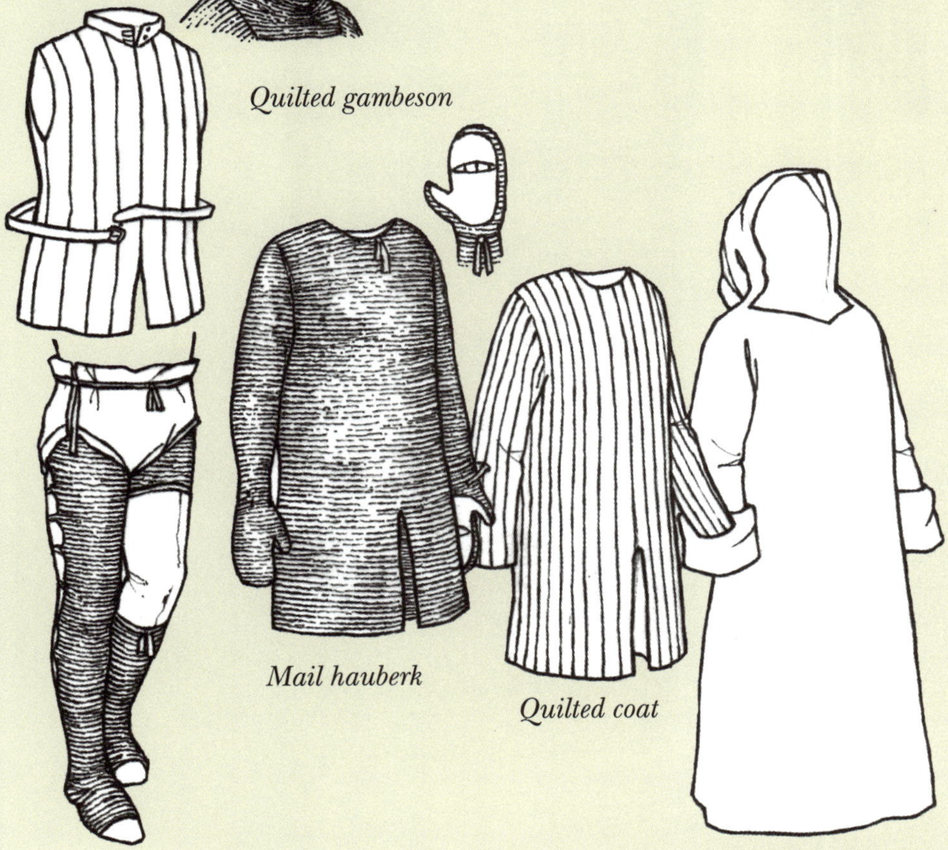

Quilted gambeson

Mail hauberk

Quilted coat

Cotton aketon

Mail armour was not solely a European innovation. This mail shirt, dating from the 15th or 16th century, is Iranian or Turkish in origin.

Fifteenth-century German mail. Riveting rings together rather than simply butting them takes longer and therefore costs more, but creates armour that is more durable and resistant to damage.

a strike. Well-fitted armour feels more tiring than heavy or restrictive, although the extra weight can be a liability. An armoured warrior who keeps moving is very difficult to bring down, as glancing blows are deflected and much of the impact is absorbed by the armour. However, as the wearer tires they are more likely to be caught flat-footed and hit with a square-on blow, or one aimed at a weak spot.

This depiction of fighting during the First Crusade (1096–99) illustrates the dangers of being immobilized, even if wearing good armour. Unhorsed knights have been slain, and others are severely imperilled after being grappled by their opponents.

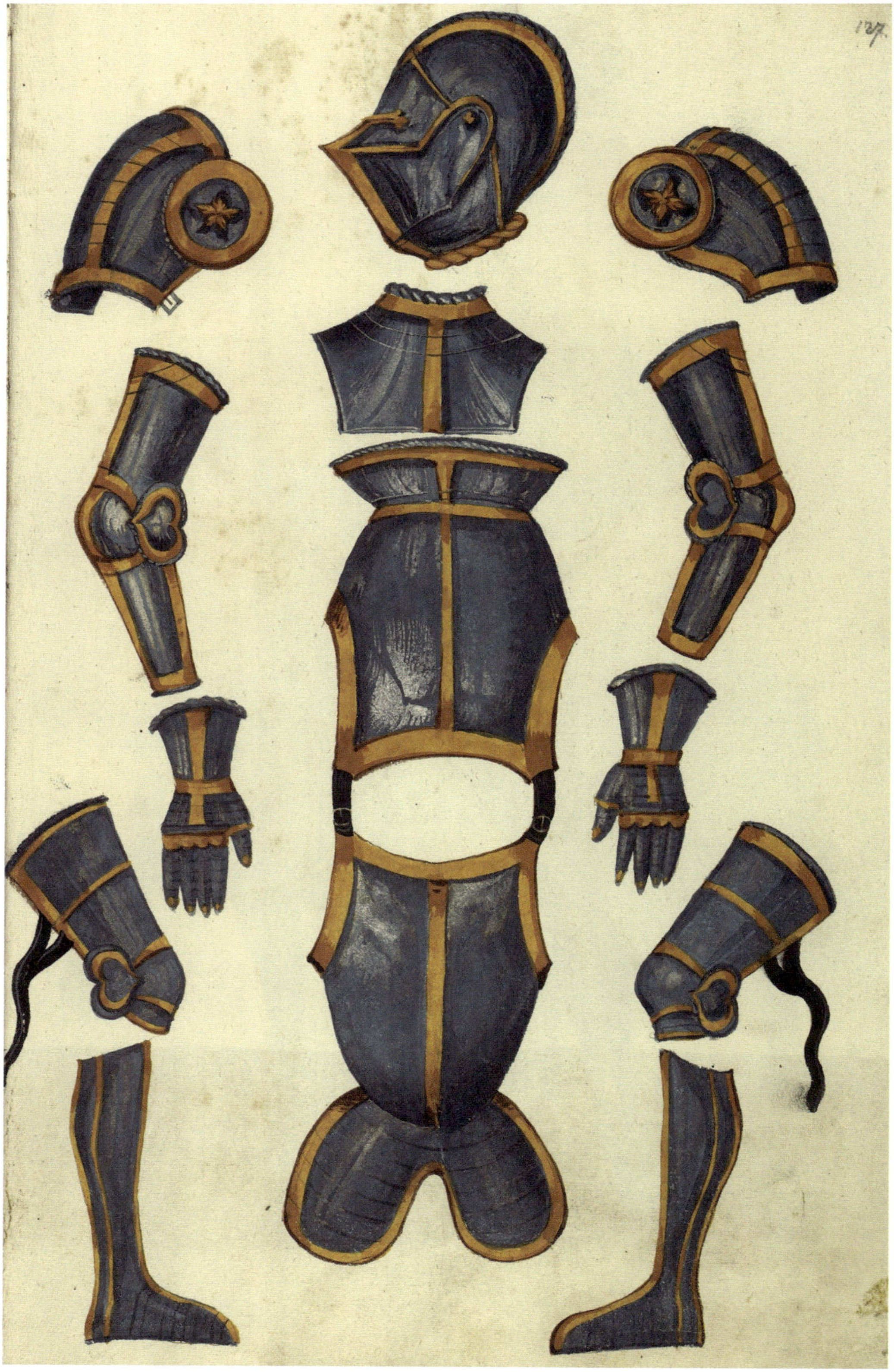
127

Opposite: This 16th century artwork shows the various elements of a typical suit of plate armour. The armour articulates at various joints to balance protection with mobility. Major points include neck, shoulders, elbows, wrists, knees and ankles. In total, a complete suit can have 20–25 articulated locations.

Right: Cuisse and poleyn – thigh and knee protectors – dating from the Late Medieval period, circa 1600CE.

A common tactic was to pull knights off their horses with a hook mounted on a pole weapon, then drag them to the ground. Specialist anti-armour weapons included knives designed to pierce narrow weak spots in plate armour. There is little the armourer could do to counter such attacks, though even when an armoured knight was pinned down by multiple assailants, finishing him off remained a difficult task.

Other risks could be mitigated by armour design as well. Originally, a 'tourney' was an informal meeting of knights who would

The human body has natural 'point traps' where a lance can fix cleanly and transfer its full force rather than sliding off. This 16th-century Austrian grandguard protects the vulnerable upper chest and neck with thicker metal, while its angled surface helps deflect the point away.

The lance rest was not particularly useful in a melee, but in a formal joust it provided an extra degree of stability and greatly improved the user's chances of a clean strike.

fight with their usual weapons to test their skill, whereas a 'joust' referred to any combat on foot or horseback. Later in the medieval era, the tourney was formalized into a grand affair with rules, and the term 'joust' came to specifically mean a mutual charge with lances.

The Gambeson

The gambeson is known by various names and has a few specialist variants, but essentially it is a thick jacket of quilted cloth, padded with whatever material might be available, such as wool or horsehair. A gambeson could be worn under other armour to provide additional protection and absorb some of the impact from blows, or worn on its own as a standalone defence.

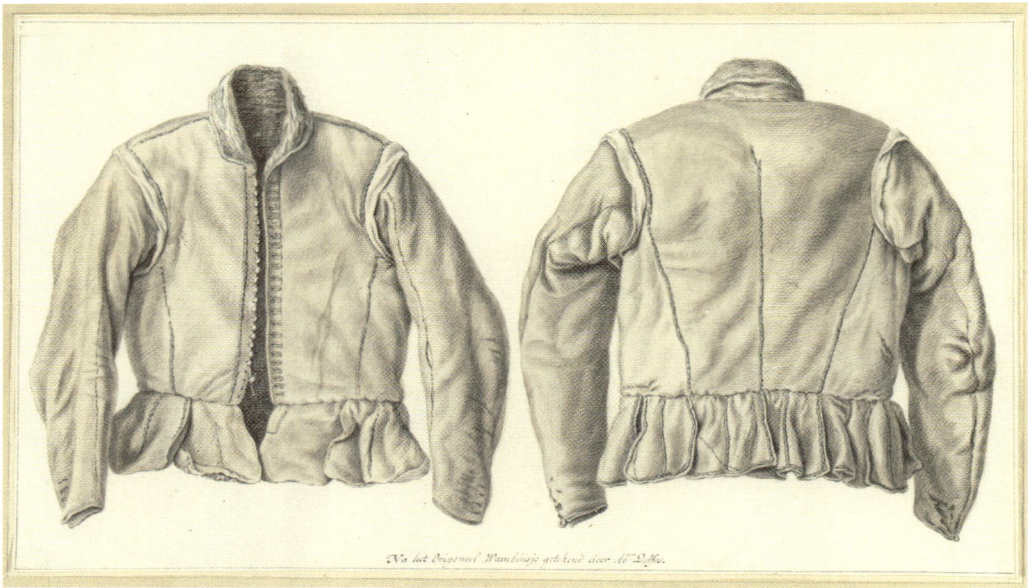

The gambeson was a key part of personal armour, providing good protection on its own. While metal could stop a weapon from penetrating and distribute the force of a blow, the gambeson's padding dissipated the force, preventing serious injuries even when the armour was not penetrated.

A gambeson provided good protection against cutting weapons and was reasonably effective against impact even without harder or more rigid armour over the top. Protection against impaling weapons and projectiles was less effective, as a point could snag on cloth but might slide off metal. Once a point had 'bitten' in this manner it was guided into the target, although the layers of closely woven cloth would still slow and entangle the weapon.

The gambeson, with or without a helmet, was the best protection a common foot soldier was likely to have. There is evidence that it could stop arrows, although not 100 per cent reliably. During the Third Crusade (1189–92), the army under King Richard I of England was forced to march from Acre to Jaffa along the coast, harassed by enemy horse archers. It was recorded that many of the foot soldiers looked like porcupines due to all the arrows embedded in their armour, yet they were still able to maintain the march. Eventually, a Crusader counterattack brought about the Battle of Arsuf in which the enemy force was driven off with heavy losses.

Leather and Hide Armour

Leather and rawhide have been used to make protective clothing throughout human history. The difference between the two is that leather has been tanned and becomes more supple, whereas rawhide – as its name suggests – is closer to its natural state. By itself, leather offers only basic protection against battlefield weapons. It is certainly better than nothing, but leather is more useful as a component in a composite piece than as armour in its own right.

Boiled leather, or cuir-bouilli, has been an effective armour type for centuries. Boiling in wax or oil hardens the leather, enabling armour makers to mould components to fit the wearer. Cuir-bouilli breastplates and limb protectors were used since ancient times and the technique remained common during the medieval period. A boiled leather armour component was lighter but less resilient than metal, and had some of the same characteristics. A blade or even an arrow striking at a poor angle might be deflected, although resistance to penetration is naturally lower than that of a metal armour component.

Rawhide offers better protection than leather, as it has not been made soft by tanning. Hide could be used to make a coat, offering protection in its own right. The 'buff coat', made of oil-tanned leather

The Battle of Arsuf (1191) during the Third Crusade was an important victory for the crusaders, having marched along the coast in high temperatures and under near-constant archery harassment. Many soldiers arrived at the battle site with multiple arrows protruding from their armour.

which has many of the characteristics of rawhide, was a popular form of protection for cavalry and foot soldiers after the end of the medieval period. Examples survive have have withstood a close-range shot from a wheel-lock pistol.

Armour of leather or hide was relatively easy to obtain, so might be in use with common foot soldiers throughout the medieval period. However, leather and hide were most effective when used to create composite armour such as brigandine or as a backing for mail. Composite armours typically used metal plates, discs or rings, but boiled leather could be substituted for these.

These peytral plates of cuir-boulli, dating from the early 16th century, formed part of the protection given to a warhorse, protecting its chest and shoulders.

Brigandine

Appearing in the late 1300s, Brigandine is a composite armour created by riveting small metal plates to a coat of rawhide, leather or cloth. It may or may not have a second layer of cloth, creating a sandwich of metal. Brigandine is sometimes misunderstood to be 'studded leather' armour, since the rivet heads are visible outside the leather or cloth layer. In fact, it is much more effective than a leather jerkin with a few studs would be.

Brigandine offers the advantages of both hard and soft armour. It is reasonably flexible but may turn aside a blow that strikes one of the plates. In this it is most effective against cutting and lighter blunt weapons, turning aside a sharp edge and distributing force. Impaling attacks are more likely to cause injury.

Easier to make than mail, and therefore cheaper, brigandine developed from an earlier form of armour known as a coat of plates, which appeared around 1200CE. Some users augmented their brigandine with pieces of rigid armour such as arm guards. Examples ranged from simple brigandines for use by common foot soldiers to elaborately decorated examples worn as much for show as for protection by those who could afford them.

A similar garment was the jack, or jack of plates, which had metal plates sewn rather than riveted between layers of cloth. Crude forms of the jack could be put together by almost anyone, with plates sewn only into the most vital areas in some cases. Armour of this type remained in use into the Renaissance and could be worn in circumstances where overt 'battle' armour was inappropriate. The wearer of a fashionable

An Italian brigandine from around 1400, of a sort used by Venetian soldiers operating in the Aegean region. Venice controlled a vast trade empire and was a major player in European politics despite not being a kingdom in the conventional sense.

An Italian brigandine plate, circa 1400–50. Plates like this were sandwiched between layers of cloth to form a type of composite armour that, while less effective than articulated plate, was more affordable.

brigandine or jack had a significant advantage over an impoverished assailant whose clothing offered vastly less protection.

Chain Mail

Chain mail, also called mail, or *maille*, is constructed from metal rings riveted or butted together. It is thought to have been invented by the ancient Celts. To make chain mail it is necessary to have access to metal

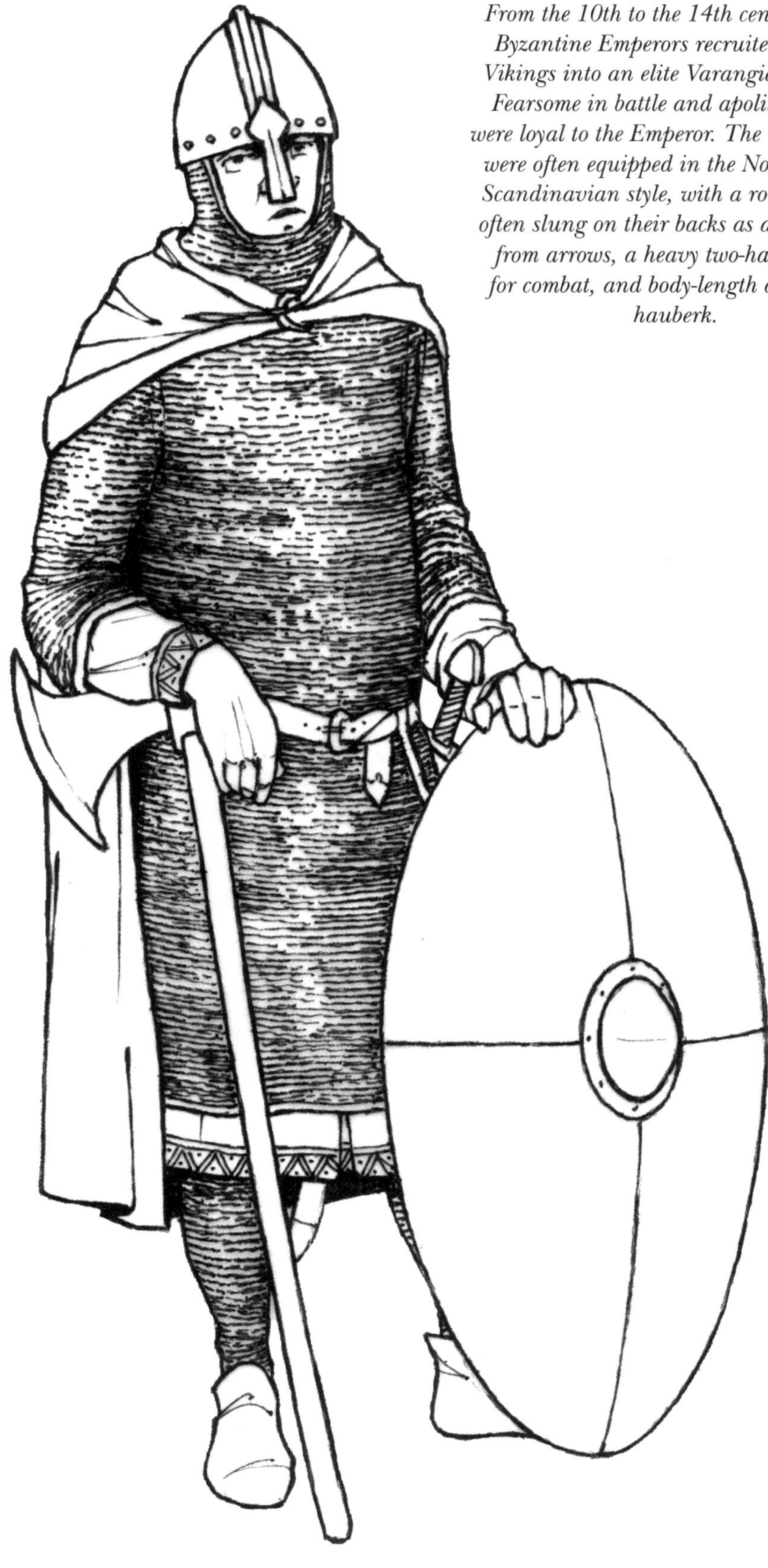

From the 10th to the 14th centuries, the Byzantine Emperors recruited selected Vikings into an elite Varangian Guard. Fearsome in battle and apolitical, they were loyal to the Emperor. The Varangians were often equipped in the Norman and Scandinavian style, with a round shield often slung on their backs as a protection from arrows, a heavy two-handed axe for combat, and body-length chainmail hauberk.

wire, which was difficult to manufacture in the ancient world. Wire was made by a process called riving, in which the metal was drawn through a series of increasingly small holes and thereby stretched out into wire. This was a time-consuming procedure undertaken by apprentice smiths as part of their training.

Once wire of a suitable thickness was available, it was formed into rings by winding around a suitably sized rod then cut along the length

An Italian brigandine from the early 16th century.

A mail shirt of Syrian or Turkish origin from the early 16th century.

of the rod. Rings were then interlocked, usually with each linking to four others, and either butted or riveted together. Butted rings were hammered so that their ends met tightly together, but receiving a heavy blow force them apart again. A rivet through the ends of each ring created a more durable piece of armour but increased the time required to produce it.

Individual rings of mail can shift slightly, improving flexibility and helping to disperse the force of a blow. However, mail armour does not distribute its weight evenly across the body, which can make it feel heavier than its actual mass.

A mail sleeve from 16th-century Germany. Even after the development of fully articulated plate armour, mail remained useful for protecting complex or hard-to-cover parts of the body.

Creating what is essentially a chain mail blanket is relatively straightforward, but shaping the armour to fit the contours of a human demands greater skill. Mail armour that was too big added needless weight and could impede the wearer. Typically, mail was formed into a shirt or coat, although some cultures used it in different ways. There is evidence of Norse warriors wearing a mail hood, which draped over the shoulders, rather than using their mail as body protection. Combined

Ottoman mail armour from the 16th or 17th century, featuring a mail coif to protect the head. The coif consists of a metal calotte (skullcap) with mail curtains attached.

MAIL COIF

Mail was also used to protect smaller or more awkward areas that were difficult to cover with metal plates, and to supplement other armour. The mail coif, thought to have appeared in the 900s, was essentially a mail hood of interlinked rings worn beneath or in place of a helmet. On its own, however, a coif offered little protection, as any force passing through it could still jar the skull and brain. For this reason is was typically worn over padding to help reduce the impact of blows.

Later, the coif was replaced by the aventail, a piece of mail hanging from the rear of the helm to protect the neck. Mail face guards were also used with open-face helms. This idea was revived as late as World War I, when tank crews were given mail face guards to protect against spallation – hot metal fragments that broke off the inside of a tank's armour when struck by bullets. Today, chain mail is still used to protect divers from shark bites, as well as butcher and fish processors who work with sharp knives.

with a shield, this covered all the likely targets an opponent might strike without the weight or complexity of a mail coat.

Mail was usually worn over a gambeson or similar padded garment to cushion blows, though heavy bruising was still possible. Bones dating from the Early Medieval period have been discovered showing the imprint of mail rings, suggesting that the force of a blow was transmitted to the bone – and that the wearer survived the impact.

During the Early Medieval period, the usual armour for heavy cavalry was a mail hauberk (or byrnie), which covered the torso and upper parts of the limbs. For the Norman cavalry that conquered England after 1066, the hauberk was typically combined with a helm and sturdy boots. While this offered only partial protection – especially because the hauberk was split at the front and back to permit riding a horse – when combined with a large kite shield, it made a Norman knight extremely difficult to bring down.

A hauberk of this type was heavy, but its greater issue was poor weight distribution. The weight of the hauberk fell mostly on the shoulders and hips, making it more tiring to wear than other forms of armour with a similar weight and protection.

Some users preferred a smaller and lighter mail torso protector known as the habergeon, or mail shirt. This continued to be used even after the hauberk ceased to be the primary battlefield armour. A mail shirt could be concealed under bulky clothing and worn in situations where full battle armour was impractical. Other variations on mail armour included the jazerant, which emerged in the Middle East during the 11th to 12th centuries. This consisted of mail sewn between layers of cloth for added protection.

Lamellar and Scale Armour

Lamellae are small rectangular plates made from metal, cuir bouilli, bone, stiffened rawhide or other rigid materials. These plates are laced together in an overlapping pattern to create armour that can be worn on its own or layered over other protection, such as mail. Lamellar armour is not especially difficult to make and can be repaired by removing and

Lamellar armour is formed from small individual metal plates (lamellae) fastened together to create a flexible garment. This example is thought to be Tibetan and dates from the 16th or 17th century.

replacing damaged lamellae. However, this is a time-consuming process since a large amount of lacing has to be undone in order to access a single lamella.

There is evidence of lamellar armour being used by the ancient Assyrians, and it remained popular during the Byzantine Empire (330–1453CE). It was also employed by various groups across Europe during the Early Medieval period. Lamellar is closely related to scale armour, which uses small plates, or scales, attached to a backing of cloth or leather. This is a key difference between the two: the components of lamellar armour are attached to one another whereas scales are fixed to a backing material. Like lamellar, scale armour was in use for centuries.

The heavy cavalry of the Byzantine Empire made extensive use of scale – as well as chain and lamellar – armour to protect both horse and rider. These cataphracts were Eastern counterparts of mounted knights who fought in a broadly similar manner, although they generally operated alongside lightly equipped horse archers. Cataphract cavalry were used throughout the region by many powers, with a history stretching back to Roman times. Although their armour and equipment changed over the centuries, the basic concept of a charge to scatter enemy infantry did not. The momentum of the armoured horse and rider was a weapon in and of itself; accounts survive of enemy infantrymen sent flying by the impact of a charge.

Opposite: Unlike European lamellar designs, Japanese armour addressed the same challenges in a different way. This do-maru *(cuirass) is made of lacquered scales of leather, with the shoulders and arms protected by separate, detachable pieces.*

Plate Armour

Plate armour refers to any type constructed from large rigid plates, including, for example, breastplates or limb guards fashioned from cuir-bouilli. However, the term is most commonly associated

A depiction of a king's death from a late 13th- or early 14th-century Bible. The battling knights are shown wearing contemporary armour and weapons, even though the scene illustrates an event from the Old Testament.

with the articulated plate worn by Western knights during the High and Late Medieval periods. Arguably, in a broader sense, the Roman *lorica segmentata* could also be considered a form of plate armour, although many would not recognize it as such.

LATE PERIOD PLATE ARMOUR

Kasten-brust armour, characterized by its boxy or curved breastplate, was popular around 1400–50. However, the classic form of plate armour is Gothic plate, which reached its peak in the late 1400s. Influenced by the style of the Gothic architectural period (circa 1200–1500), this armour is distinguished by fluting that is both decorative and functional. The multiple curves on the armour surface help to deflect blows while reinforcing the strength of the plate overall.

Maximilian armour was largely similar in design to Gothic plate. The name is a modern designation, likely inspired by the style's popularity during the reign of Emperor Maximilian I of the Holy Roman Empire (1493–1519). The fluting of this armour style grew denser and more intricate between 1520 and 1535, whereas earlier Maximilian armour was less fluted.

Mail, sometimes reinforced or augmented with small plates or strips of armour, was the primary heavy protection used in Western Europe until the early 14th century. The techniques of articulating plates were known before this but were not in widespread practice.

Plate armour had numerous advantages over mail, notably that it was more protective for the same weight of metal. Well-shaped plate was likely to deflect a blow to some extent, whereas a pointed weapon could force mail rings apart and penetrate the armour.

Opposite: Thirteenth century Russian mail armour reinforced with lamellae over the ribs and vital organs. Easier to produce than fully articulated plate, this type of armour still gave protection.

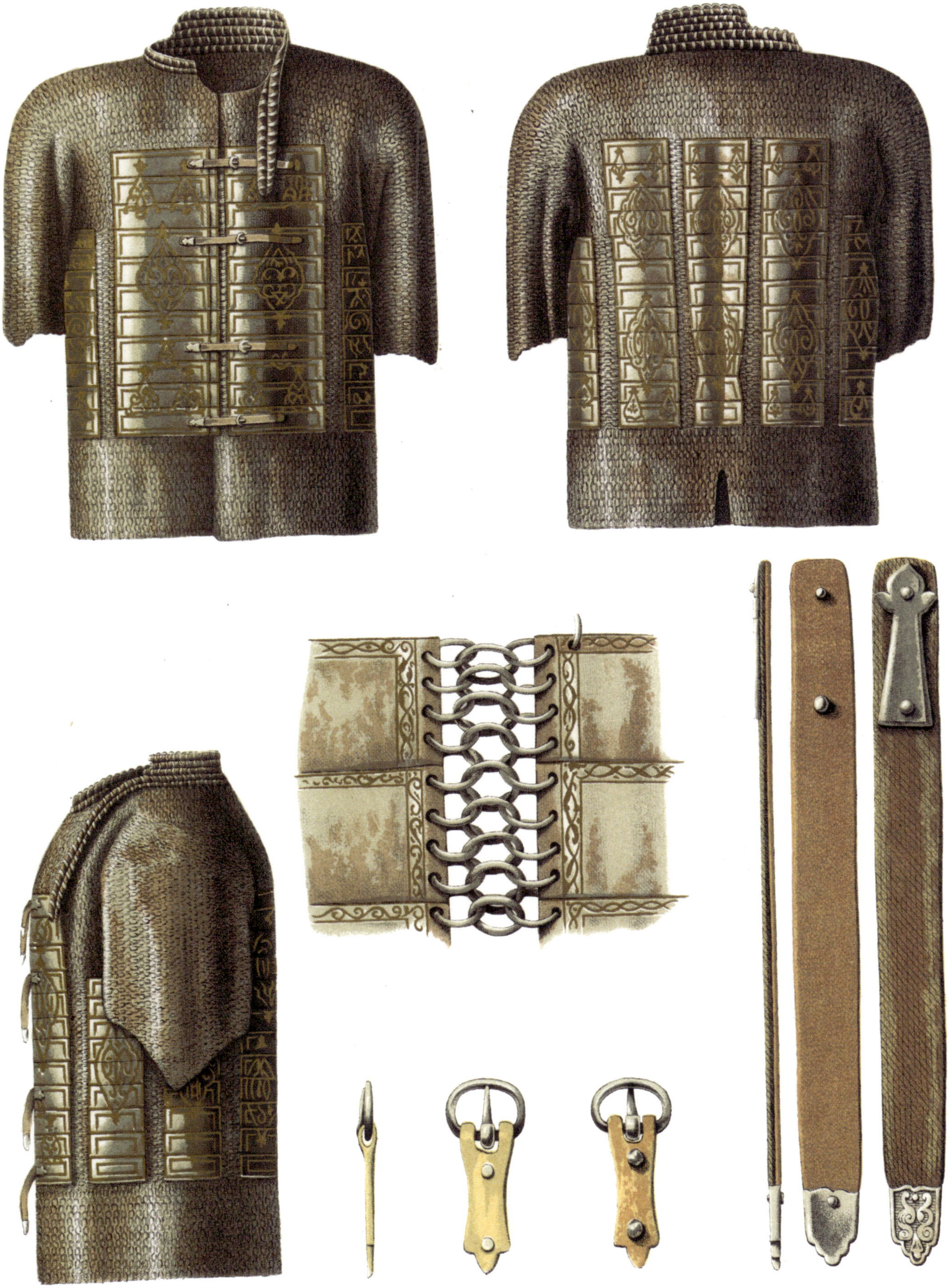

EUROPEAN KNIGHT (1400)

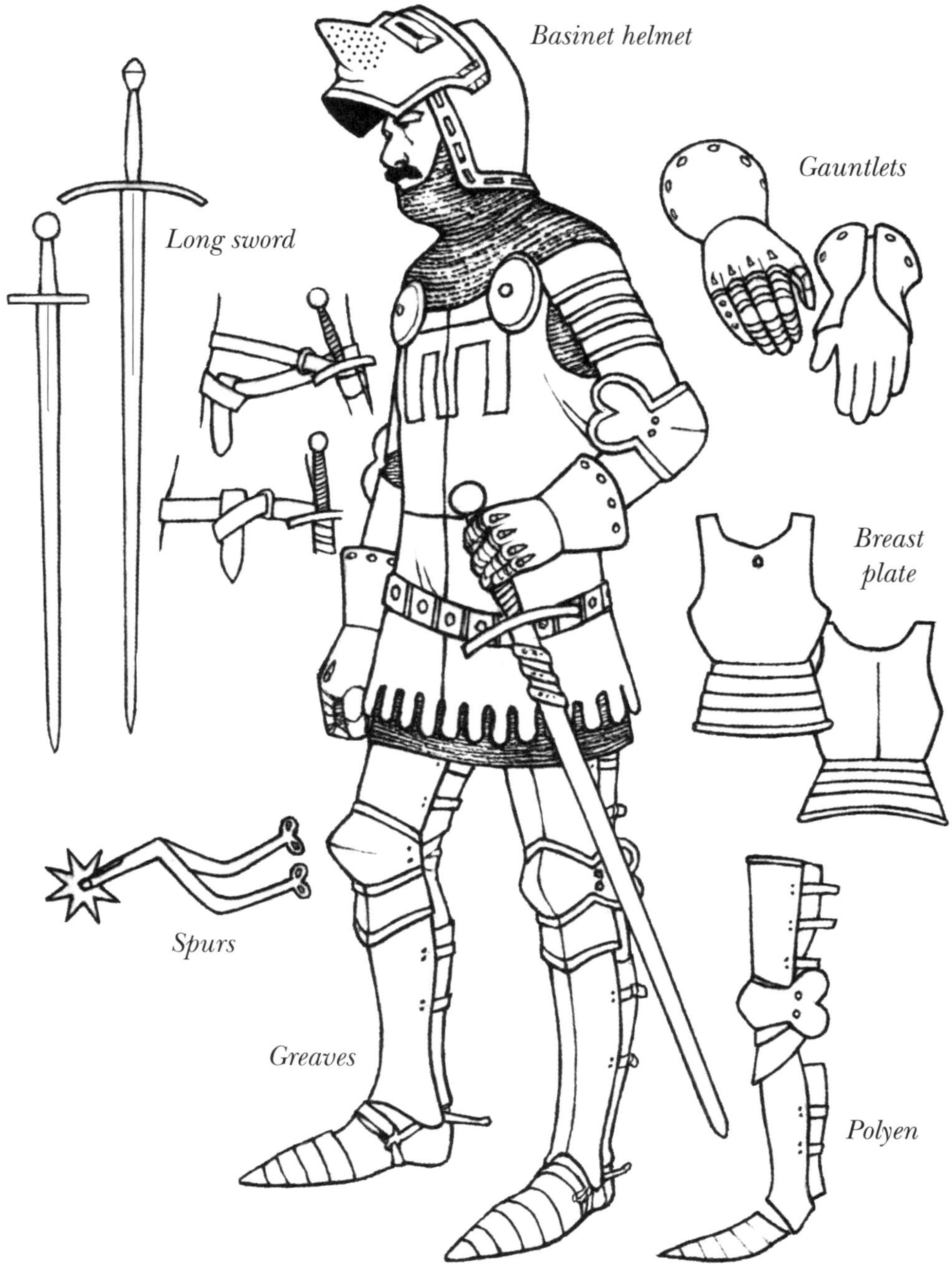

By the fifteenth century, plate armour was in widespread use, with mail normally used to cover joints and weak points rather than providing the main protection. This knight is protected by a mail-backed breastplate and plate limb armour. His visored helm allows him to see and breathe freely when not in combat but offers rigid protection for his face. The basic weaponry of the knight, i.e. sword and lance, had not changed but an array of axes, maces and picks were used in combat, in an effort to punch through the improved protection that plate armour offered.

An armour suit reconstructed from components found in the ruined Venetian fortress at Chalcis. The chest is protected by a brigandine, while gaps in the plate armour on the limbs are filled with chain mail.

The move to articulated plate armour was gradual, with various 'transitional armours' appearing during the 13th and 14th centuries. Initially these were made of mail, augmented by plate pieces, but developed until plate had become the primary material and mail was relegated to covering weak points.

Full plate armour did not become common until the 15th century. Despite this, many period dramas and pseudo-medieval fantasy movies portray warriors from much earlier times wearing full plate, fuelling the enduring image of the 'knight in shining armour' as synonymous with the medieval era. Illustrationns of the King Arthur myth, for example, routinely depict knights in battle against Saxons around 800CE as clad in armour that would not appear for until seven centuries later.

Armour of this kind could withstand the firearms of its time, and by the mid to late 1400s, partial plate was available even for common foot soldiers. Spanish conquistadors, for example, wore a breastplate and helmet combination, and historical sword-fighting systems include techniques aimed at the armpits and knees – areas left exposed by armour. Heavy cavalry used half-plate in the wars of the Renaissance, and although its use gradually declined, it remained fashionable for portraits. This has contributed to the mistaken impression that medieval-style armour remained in use for longer than it actually did.

Other Forms of Armour

Ring armour, or ring mail, is theoretically a form of reinforced leather or hide armour, in which metal rings are sewn directly onto a

This 15th-century Iranian mail shirt is constructed mostly from iron links, with copper alloy rings incorporated along the sleeves and edges. The armour is further imbued with divine protection, featuring the names of Allah and the five great Imams stamped into the rings.

OTTOMAN CAVALRY ARMOUR (1400)

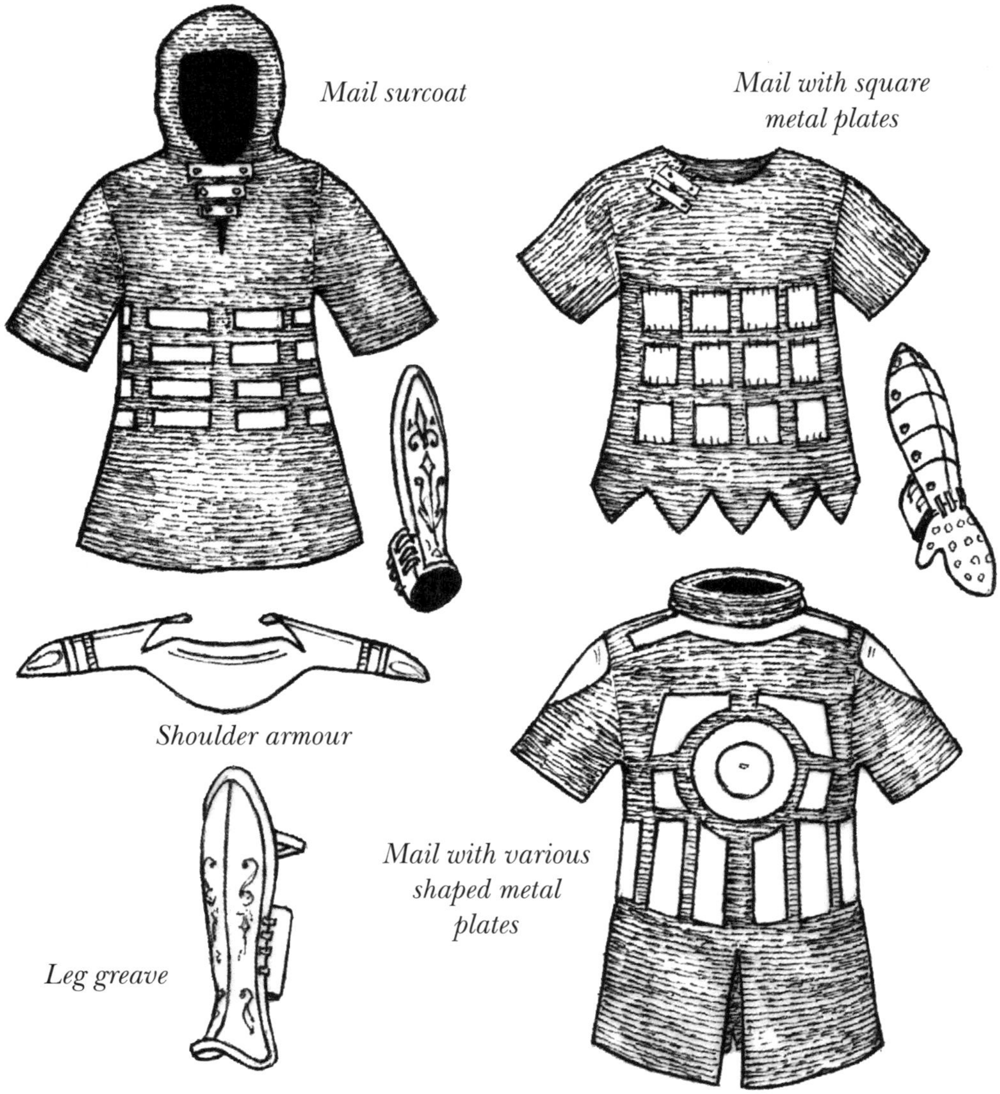

Muslim armies continued to use mail as the main protective component in their armour after it had fallen out of favour in the West. Mail was often reinforced by small plates or scales at critical points, improving the protection of what was generally lighter armour than that used by Western knights. The protection used by both groups reflected their fighting styles. The Westerners preferred to act as a battering ram while the Muslim cavalry were more mobile. Lack of a tradition of jousting with the lance was probably a factor in the continued use of flexible mail rather than a move to rigid plate.

PLATED ARMOUR

Plated mail is a variation on traditional mail, consisting mainly of interlinked rings with small metal plates added for extra protection. It was most commonly used in Eastern Europe and the Middle East, giving it a distinctively 'eastern' appearance. In the West, ailettes served a similar purpose. These were small armour pieces of cuir-bouilli or metal, attached to the shoulders to help defend against downward blows.

backing material. This concept is logical: metal rings provide a hard outer layer to disperse the force of a strike or prevent penetration by point or edge, while the padded backing cushions the impact. However, evidence suggests that this type of ring armour was not actually used in Europe, and its supposed existence was likely inferred from misunderstood historical sources.

One of the sources often cited is the Bayeux Tapestry, which depicts the Norman invasion of England. It seems that what was once identified as 'ring mail' in the tapestry is in fact a stylized representation of chain mail. Tapestries are not photorealistic, after all. While it remains possible that such armour existed somewhere at some point, no archaeological evidence has been found to support it.

Similarly, armour known as 'banded mail' is of questionable historical authenticity. Much of what is widely accepted as fact about historical armour and weaponry originates from the 19th century.

EXER CI TU:

Some interpretations of the Bayeux Tapestry have been cited to support the existence of ring mail. In the tapestry, Norman knights wearing chain or ring armour are shown fighting Anglo-Saxon warriors who appear to be similarly equipped.

Although this period produced some valuable research, several misconceptions became widely accepted. One is the belief that historical warriors could wield enormous or extremely heavy weapons. This idea likely arose from the survival of oversized 'parade weapons' and decorative or commemorative pieces, rather than from actual battlefield use.

Conversely, splinted armour did exist. Consisting of strips of metal or other hard material applied over a backing, it was generally used to fashion lower leg and arm protection. Gauntlets could also be reinforced with narrow strips of metal, providing additional protection to the hands and wrists without requiring fully articulated construction.

Above: King Gunther von Schwartzburg, claimant to the throne of the Holy Roman Empire, depicted wearing splinted limb protection, in an illustration dated circa 1330.

Opposite: A fine late example of German fluted armour, dating from 1535. Although providing almost comprehensive cover of the body, the back of the thighs remained exposed for mobility reasons, and therefore vulnerable.

Those that could afford it commissioned specialized armour for different purposes. This 16th-century half-armour, for example, was designed for use in tournament fighting on foot.

CHAPTER 3

Armour Components

A FULL SUIT OF ARMOUR is sometimes called a 'harness' or, using the much older term, a 'panoply', a word that has since come to describe an impressive collection of items. A knight's panoply certainly was impressive, and also vastly expensive. In addition to the purchase cost, it had to be maintained, which required the services of specialist craftsmen. A rich knight might own multiple suits of armour, each tailored for different situations. Those unable to afford separate armour for the tourney and for battle could still adapt a single harness, adding, removing, or substituting components to suit the occasion.

Shields

Although not a piece of armour as such, a shield was an essential part of a warrior's equipment for much of the medieval era. Later, when armour had developed to the point where most weapons were ineffective against it, a knight might dispense with the shield in favour of a heavy two-handed weapon. However, for much of the period the shield was an important and effective adjunct to the knight's armour.

The civilizations of ancient Greece and the eastern Mediterranean relied heavily on large, bowl-shaped shields to protect their close-order infantry. Personal armour was optional, but a well-designed shield was essential to survival in phalanx warfare.

The gold and ivory shield of Philip II of Macedon, father of Alexander the Great. Philip II was a great military innovator, who adapted the equipment and weaponry of his heavy infantry to boost their flexibility and effectiveness in battle.

Shields were primarily constructed from wood, usually with a metal frame. Some designs used rawhide to increase resilience. Later in the medieval period, a shield also served as a form of personal banner, displaying heraldic symbols to identify the user. Even before this decoration was common, shields displayed family, tribal or religious symbols. A shield could be used passively, simply being raised in the hope that a blow would strike it, but a skilled fighter could employ it far more effectively. A shield could be used to shut down an opponent's weapon by shoving it into him and pinning his arm, or to intercept a blow such that the user's arm struck the shield face. It could also conceal the user's intentions, with a chambered weapon hidden by the shield until the moment came to strike. Pushing the shield into the path of a stroke would foreshorten the weapon's arc and render a blow less effective.

A trade-off existed between shield size and effectiveness. A large shield protected more of the body but was harder to use actively due to its weight and bulk. Conversely, a smaller shield offered less protection against arrows. Shape was also a factor. Shields used by early medieval warriors who largely fought on foot tended to be round, whereas those

The buckler resembles an overgrown shield boss and provides little passive protection. However, in the hands of a skilled user the buckler becomes a second weapon that can also be used defensively. This example dates from 16th-century Persia.

Bas relief of a Roman soldier, equipped in the characteristic style with large scutum *shield, body armour and helmet. The Roman shield design gradually fell out of use as the empire declined, with round shields becoming more popular among the successor kingdoms that followed.*

used on horseback could be differently shaped to extend protection to the user's legs.

In its classic period, the Roman military favoured large shields – rectangular for legionaries and oval for auxiliaries – and it is tempting to assume these designs would remain influential long after the empire's fall. While stocks of Roman equipment existed and were likely copied, as imperial authority weakened most 'Roman' troops increasingly relied on the arms and armour typical of their own regional traditions.

Round shields were widely used by both the Germanic tribes who pushed west during the Migration Period and with the Norsemen. Early 'Viking' shields were constructed of wood faced with leather. It was round in shape, and large enough to offer protection against arrows but light enough to be used offensively. Although the Norse people had some of the finest horses in Europe, their fighting style in the Early Medieval period was primarily on foot, and the need for quick embarkation and disembarkation from ships also influenced shielf design and mobility.

Later 'Viking' shields were given metal rims to make them more durable, as well as a central metal boss that could be used to strike with. The shields of the Anglo-Saxons were similar in design and size, and they fought in a similar manner. This pattern was repeated elsewhere in Europe, but as mounted combat became more prevalent there was a shift in shield design.

From the 12th century, the kite shield was replaced by the heater, whose rounded lower half was shorter than that of a kite. One reason for this was the improvement of leg protection. A heater was easier to use on

In the post-Roman world, migrating tribes settled in former imperial territories and established early medieval kingdoms. This shield boss was probably created in the kingdom of Lombardy in the 7th century.

NORMAN KITE SHIELD

The Normans, who invaded England in 1066, were originally Norsemen who had settled in northern France. Over time they adopted both the culture and the fighting style of the Franks, with the mailed horseman as the main force on the battlefield. Their shield design reflected that change, with horsemen using the long kite shield. Wide at the top with an elongated tail, the kite shield offered protection to the horseman's legs, which were not covered by armour at that time. The kite shield could be used on foot but was not as 'handy' as a round shield.

It is not accurate to claim that the Norman fighting system was superior to that of the Anglo-Saxons, as many tactical and organizational factors influenced outcomes. What is certain, however, is that the cavalry-based Norman army defeated the Anglo-Saxons and conquered England – a pattern that was generally repeated across medieval Europe.

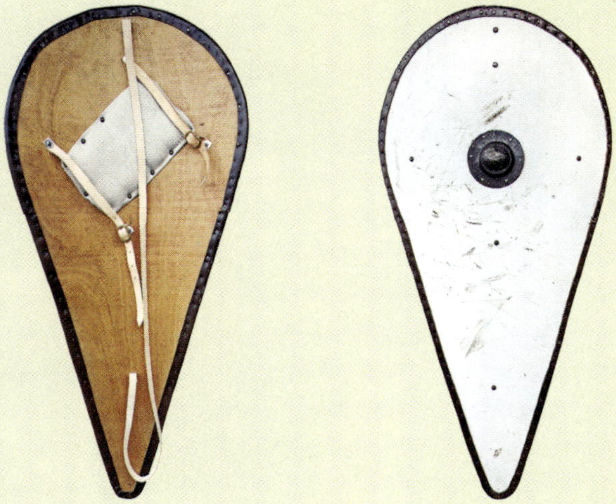

The kite shield resulted from Eastern influences on the Byzantine Empire. Although the idea that it was developed for cavalry use has been challenged, it is eminently suitable for that role.

foot, such as when attacking or defending fortifications. Formal heraldry began to develop around the same time as the heater entered popular use. Rather than a shield bearing whatever image the user preferred, standard components and rules for their use were gradually codified during the remainder of the medieval period.

The buckler, while shield-like, was used differently. Typically formed of a central bowl containing the handgrip and a small rim, bucklers might be constructed entirely of metal. They offered little protection against arrows or impaling weapons like spears, but could be highly effective against other hand weapons. A buckler can function as a weapon as well as a shield, used to strike with its rim or to confuse an opponent about the wielder's intentions.

Head Protection

The head and throat are notoriously difficult to protect, and armour must balance several factors. While deflecting blows is critically important, excessive restriction of vision or breathing can make a helmet a liability. Poor ventilation can lead to a buildup of carbon dioxide, causing discomfort or claustrophobia and reducing the quality of air drawn in, no matter how hard the wearer is breathing.

Vision presents another problem in close combat. A warrior attacked from any direction than straight ahead might fail to notice an attack coming. This is not just about being too slow to position a shield; limited awareness can also reduce the effectiveness of armour, leaving vulnerable spots exposed. Normally, a warrior would be moving in

One solution to the problem of giving good protection when needed yet allowing freedom to see and breathe was to use a composite rigid/mail construction for head protection. Various systems were used, most of which involved mail hanging from the brim of the helm and covering the wearer's neck and shoulders. Some versions had a flap that could be lifted up across the face and, in some cases, included a rigid eye guard or nasal bar.

such a way that blows landed suboptimally, making the most of armour protection. Someone blindsided by a skilled opponent would receive the full force of the blow at an optimal angle for penetration and might be taken out of action before they could turn to face the new threat.

Most helms had very narrow eye slits to minimize the risk of penetration, although they were not foolproof. An English longbowman who could not strike the head of a man-sized target at 50 yards would be considered 'but lightly esteemed' by his colleagues. That translated to a lot of arrows coming in on a nearly flat trajectory, with the law of

A sallet said to have belonged to 'Abd Allāh Muhammad.
His defeat in 1492 ended 250 years of Nasrid rule in Granada and marked the completion of the Reconquista – the Catholic reconquest of the Iberian peninsula.

The armet became common throughout Europe, with its hinged visor allowing the wearer to observe the wider situation and breathe more easily between bouts of close combat. The custom of raising the visor to be recognized is believed to be the origin of the modern military salute.

averages dictating that some would hit weak spots. Hand weapons could also penetrate. King Henry II of France received a mortal wound in 1559 when a fragment of a jousting lance went through his visor, which was jammed slightly open. He died 10 days later.

Combat is always terrifying, and to fight with limited vision, laboured breathing and dulled hearing required great courage. To enter a battle completely blind is almost beyond belief, yet King John of Bohemia, the Holy Roman Emperor, fought on the French side at the Battle of Crécy in 1346 after losing his sight. His mount was led between two knights, and by all accounts he fought bravely until he was killed.

Early Medieval Helms

A typical early medieval helm was based on a curved metal frame circling the upper head and additional structural members curving upwards to meet above the crown of the head. Curved metal segments were added to form the bowl of the helm, along with padding and any additional pieces, such as cheek guards or curtains of chain mail intended to protect the face and neck. In some regions, fighters preferred eye protection in the form of spectacles, while in others a robust nasal bar could be used to protect the face from cutting or slashing blows.

These early helmets offered good protection for the areas they covered, but were best suited to deflecting a downward blow that would hopefully skid off the sides. In this way, the energy of the blow was dispersed rather than transmitted directly to the wearer's head. Even so, a blow might concuss or disorient the user by bouncing the brain

KETTLE HELM

Kettle helms were used throughout the medieval period, typically by archers, foot soldiers and those engaged in siege warfare. However, they left certain areas vulnerable and were replaced with better protection by those who could afford it. The great helm, also known as a pot helm and a barrel helm among other names, evolved from the earlier nasal helm and reached its classic form in the mid-1200s.

around inside his skull. The neck might also be injured even if the helm withstood the blow. Helms constructed in this manner are known by various names, of which the spangenhelm is most common. The kettle helm was an alternative, although it also lacked face protection. A kettle helm took the form of a wide-brimmed hat made of metal and provided good protection from downward blows. Kettle helms were often, but not always, made from a single piece of metal and could have additional protection such as cheek pieces.

The great helm originally had a flat top, making it relatively easy to manufacture, but this proved to be a weakness. The curved sides of the helm were effective in deflecting blows, but the top could be stoved in by a heavy impact. A more rounded crown gradually became popular. The great helm was often worn over a mail coif and eveny a metal skullcap to increase protection. Protection always comes at a price. In the case of the

Opposite: An armoured knight speaks with his king, circa 1405. Leg protection had become standard by this time, and the knight is equipped with an open-faced kettle helm.

The Arundel manuscript collection features battle scenes like this one, showing armoured combat in the 14th century. With extremely limited vision, knights would have had little sense of how the wider battle was unfolding, beyond what was directly in front of them.

great helm this was restricted vision and breathing. Holes permitted air to move in and out, but here again there was a trade-off: more holes meant easier breathing but a weaker helm. Also, it was not practical to position breathing holes anywhere but the front of the helm, which was where most blows were likely to land.

Evolution of the Helm

The metal skullcap, known as a cervellière, underwent its own evolution, eventually becoming the bascinet. The bascinet protected the sides and rear of the head as well as the crown, with some examples having an attached camail of chain mail to cover the neck. Originally worn under the great helm, the bascinet ultimately replaced it.

Face protection was provided by a removable visor that enabled a knight to breathe easily and gain a better appreciation of the situation when not engaged. There are accounts of older, more experienced knights getting rid of their visors as soon as the initial clash of a battle was over. While this increased the chance of an arrow in the face, it might also give the knight an advantage over an enemy whose restricted breathing had tired him, or who did not see a blow coming from his flank.

During the early 1400s, the camail was replaced by a plate gorget, granting improved protection to the neck and throat. This configuration became known as the great bascinet, although specific equivalents had their own names. Over the next century the bascinet evolved further into the armet, whose attached visor gave rise to the modern military salute. As knights approached a dignitary it was customary to raise the visor so that their faces could be seen, in case impostors were using their insignia to attempt an assassination.

The armet typically had a reinforced brow section and a rib running front-to-back over the crown. This not only helped deflect blows but also produced a stronger helm than a bowl shape. As with other helms, many regional and cultural variants appeared. An alternative to

the armet was the close helm. Where an armet had hinged cheek pieces, a close helm featured a full visor.

The sallet seems to have emerged in Italy in the late 1300s. Originally it was a simple helmet whose shaping was intended to protect

Opposite: Relatively simple to make, the great helm offered strong protection against frontal blows, but remained vulnerable to strikes delivered to the crown of the head.

Above: A great bascinet dating from 16th-century England. Its projecting lower face protection reduced the likelihood of a weapon penetrating the eye slits.

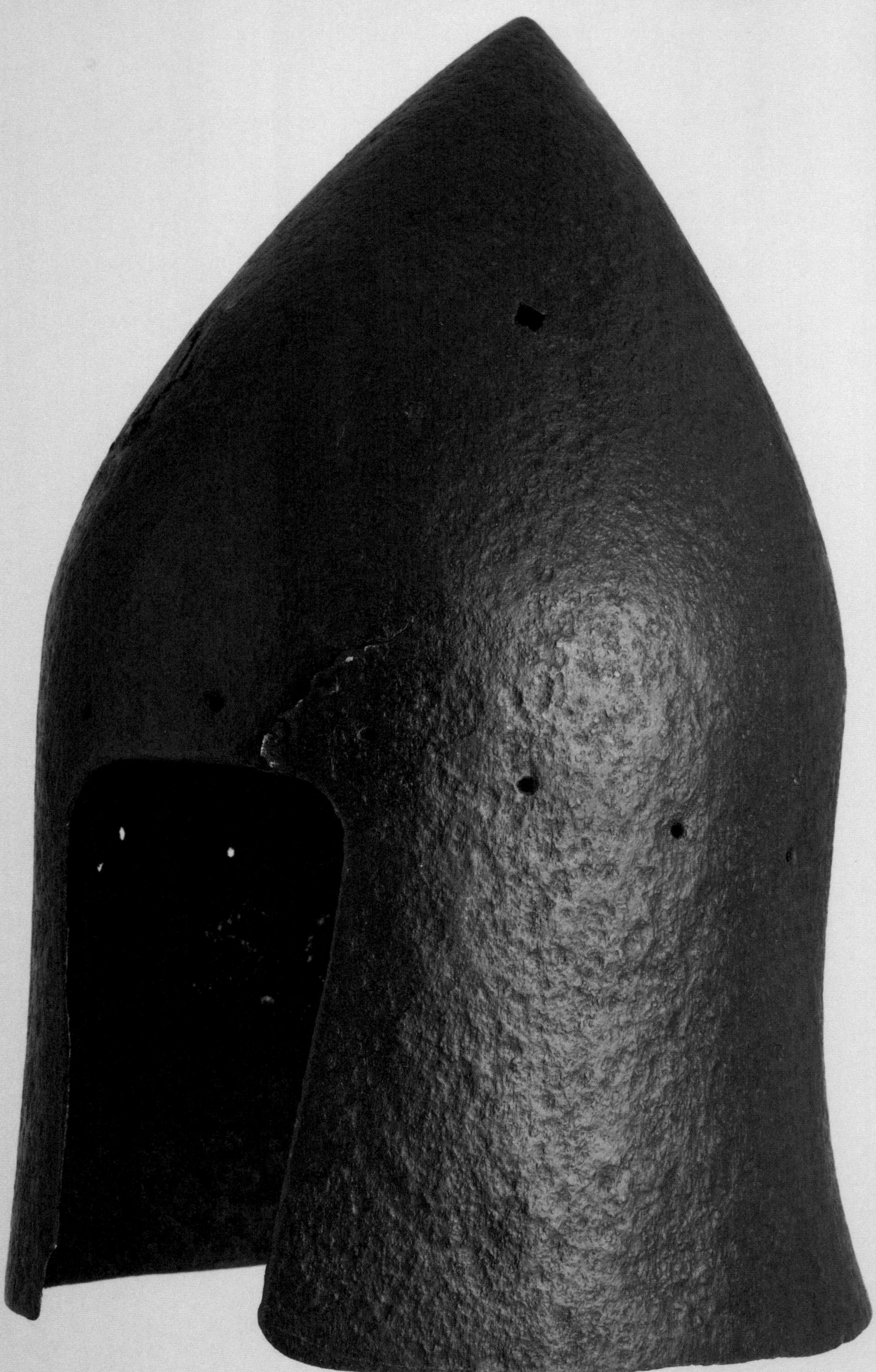

BURGONET

The burgonet, also known as a Burgundian sallet, appeared in the 1500s. Although not as protective, the burgonet was lighter and easier to produce, and interfered less with breathing and vision. As the nature of warfare changed during the Renaissance, lighter helms continued to develop with local variations, and fully enclosed designs were gradually abandoned. For example, the utilitarian 'lobster pot' helmets of the English Civil War period offered effective protection against contemporary threats while being far lighter than a full sallet or armet.

the face and neck in the absence of a camail or other attachments. The lower edges of the sallet were flared outwards to catch and deflect blows that would otherwise strike vulnerable areas. In this form, it was favoured by lightly equipped troops, while armoured cavalry tended to use a more comprehensive version. These heavier sallets typically had reinforcing plates, a visor and a separate neck guard known as a bevor.

Armouring the Torso

At first glance torso armour may appear easy to produce, as the torso has relatively large, long surfaces that can be covered by single pieces of armour. However, there are many complications. Armour must not impair the wearer's ability to twist and bend at the waist, or to ride a horse.

Opposite: A simple bascinet dating from 1375–1400. The shape of the helmet, more than the thickness of its metal, was essential in protecting the head by deflecting and dispersing the force of a blow.

A 12th-century battle scene depicted in a fresco at the castle of Sabbionara in northern Italy. Despite its importance as a status symbol, the sword is largely a secondary weapon. Combatants faced more serious threats from arrows and spears.

The shoulder and hip joints have to be protected but not restricted, and the chest must be able to expand and contract while breathing hard under exertion. Armour must not only resist penetration but also reduce the effects of blunt force trauma that could incapacitate the wearer.

The easiest way to meet all these requirements is to use flexible protection in the form of mail or cloth. However, weight and bulk distribution can be poor. To be effective, cloth or leather – whether worn as primary protection or as padding under mail – needs to be thick enough to cushion a blow or to resist penetration. This can impair movement, especially if ill-fitting armour bunches under the arms.

Opposite: A medieval German artisan makes a mail hauberk. While some elements, such as fashioning the metal rings, could be handled by apprentices, it required an expert craftsman to shape armour to fit properly.

Above: The armpit is awkward to armour and can act as a 'trap' for a thrusting weapon. If penetrated, a fatal injury is likely. To guard this vulnerable spot, small pieces of mail were used to cover the gaps between articulated plates.

The coat of mail was a well-developed technology at the start of the medieval period, with two main types. The hauberk typically had long sleeves of mail and skirts that covered the thighs, while a habergeon covered only the upper arms and left the legs uncovered. Both had advantages and drawbacks. While a hauberk offered better overall protection, it was heavier and hindered movement in battle.

Mail had to be loose enough to move in, so it hung from the body rather than fitted closely to it. The sleeves – and especially the long skirts of a hauberk – could continue moving after the wearer had stopped, creating drag and extra weight at the beginning and end of each motion. This produced both noise and a slight loss of control. When wielding weapons such as swords, where precise edge alignment is essential for an effective strike, even minor inaccuracies could reduce the power and efficiency of a blow.

The shoulders and armpits are major weak points in any torso armour. It is difficult to provide sufficient protection inside the armpit to stop a thrusting weapon, making it a natural 'blade trap' even when an opponent is not deliberately aiming there. Raising the arm to strike exposes this vulnerable point and may stretch out flexible armour, making it easier to penetrate. Some torso armour had gaps under the arms to allow freer movement, forcing the wearer to rely on a gambeson for protection in those areas.

Opposite: The brass of Sir Robert de Bures shows him wearing a mail coif and mittens. Although often depicted in fiction as a mail hood, the coif was worn over padded backing to prevent the force of a blow from being transmitted directly through the armour to the skull.

The shoulders are mostly vulnerable to blunt force from downwards blows. Even a spent stroke, glancing from the helmet, could break the collarbone, effectively disabling the warrior's arm. Flexible armour might prevent penetration yet still fail to stop serious injury. It was therefore logical that shoulder pieces were added as armour evolved. Among these was the pixane, or mantle. This was an additional layer of mail in the form of a broad collar covering the shoulders, upper chest and back.

The coat of plates was a transitional armour type constructed from small plates fixed to a mail coat. It grew in popularity throughout the 1200s but by the middle of the next century a solid breastplate had become more common than multiple plates. A breastplate, or back-and-breastplate, represented greater protection over an equivalent weight of mail, although it had its limitations.

The term for a back-and-breastplate, cuirass, is derived from the Latin word for leather, as cuirasses

Right: Mail rings from 15th-century Germany. Rings could be simply butted closed, but riveting them together provided better protection.

SHOULDERS AND ARMPITS

During the 1300s, spaulders came into widespread use. Typically made from a single curved plate of metal, they covered the shoulders but offered no protection to the armpit or upper arms. The pauldron evolved from the spaulder, incorporating overlapping lames (small plates) to cover the upper arm. These were articulated to allow free movement of the arm. The armpit was normally protected by mail, with additional reinforcing pieces often added.

Known as besagews, these were plates of varying sizes, usually more or less round, designed to protect the armpit in most positions. Some were large enough to protect part of the shoulder joint and upper arm from frontal blows. As with all armour, however, their use involved a compromise. An armour piece large enough to provide complete coverage from every angle would have to be so substantial that it would significantly impair movement.

were originally made from hardened leather. The medieval version was shaped the same but constructed of hammered metal with the two large plates connected by straps. It is relatively easy to protect the chest and upper back with a solid plate, providing the user does not gain or lose much weight. A curved single plate was more likely to shed a weapon point, deflecting it instead of receiving its full force, although there were still weak points at the shoulders and armpits.

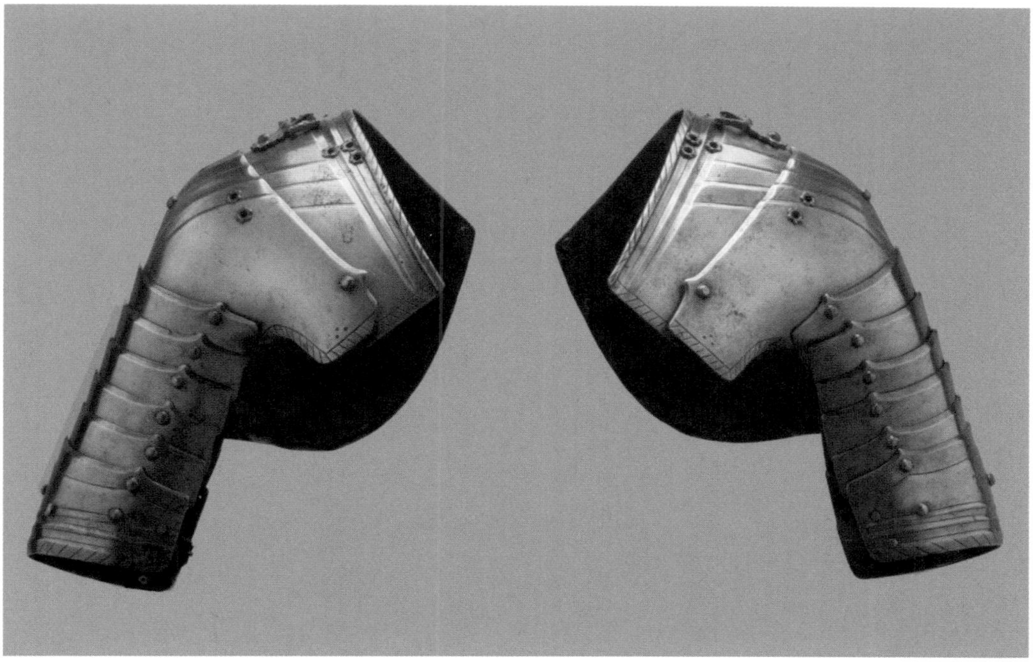

A pair of pauldrons intended for tournament use, dating from around 1500. Articulation of relatively small pieces of armour was much simpler than creating a whole suit.

Firearm Protection

With the advent of firearms, the combination of a cuirass and helmet became popular not only among mounted nobles but also among ordinary infantry, since musket balls were more likely to hit the torso than the limbs. At the close of the 15th century, the first Spanish conquistadors carried this equipment to the New World, effectively transplanting late medieval warfare into an entirely new environment.

The conquistadors quickly discovered that their armour was excessive in this new theatre of war. The heat was oppressive, and the obsidian-edged Aztec macuahuitl, or sword-club, could be stopped just as effectively by a linen or leather cuirass as by metal. Another surprise awaited in the Philippines, where warriors armed with

Tomb effigy of a knight in Gothic armour (French, Clermont-Ferrand, ca. 1425). This effigy depicts a knight wearing Gothic plate armour, including fluted and articulated plates that protect the abdomen, chest, shoulders and arms.

wooden weapons met the invaders in waist-deep surf where armour could prove a liability.

In Europe, however, the trend moved towards more and heavier armour. The cuirass could be reinforced similarly to a chain coat, reducing vulnerability of the shoulders and armpits. The waist, however, remained problematic, as the wearer needed to bend and twist freely even when not mounted. One solution was to hang mail from the bottom of the breastplate to protect the lower abdomen and legs, although armour makers gradually developed better alternatives.

Protecting the Abdomen

The plackart resembled a half-breastplate that covered the belly. It might be worn with a cuirass as reinforcement or attached to it in a way that allowed some movement. The lower abdomen was protected by faulds: a series of horizontal lames attached to the lower surface of the torso armour. The ability of faulds to concertina over one another enabled the user to retain mobility, although the groin area was vulnerable.

Mail provided essential protection, and many warriors turned necessity into a statement by wearing an armoured codpiece designed safeguard while also projecting an intimidating appearance. The hip and thigh were protected by tassets, separate plates attached to the faulds or the cuirass, while the lower back and buttocks were protected by a culet, constructed similarly to the faulds. The culet was effective against most attacks, but a knight who stood up in his stirrups to deliver a downward stroke was vulnerable to an attack under the skirts of his armour.

Shaffron and crinet – horse's head and neck defences (1480). This is a rare example of a late Gothic shaffron preserved with its matching crinet. Only a very senior knight would be able to afford this level of protection for his mount.

Above: A gorget from Germany, dating to around 1525.

The neck of a combatant was another potential vulnerable spot. Many helmets incorporated neck protection in the form of chain mail, and later metal plate. A gorget, made of either padded material or metal, offered protection to the throat and neck and might be combined with a pixane for more complete coverage. Some types of gorget included a built-in bevor to protect the lower face. The falling buffe, a later development, evolved from the bevor. It consisted of overlapping lames that could be pulled down to facilitate easier breathing, and was often paired with a burgonet helm.

Opposite: A highly decorative set of composite armour, belonging to Ulrich IV von Matsch (Italy, 14th century). This suit combines chainmail and plate elements. Steel plates protect the torso and limbs, while the knight wears a basinet style helmet.

MILANESE ARMOUR (15TH CENTURY)

By the fifteenth century, plate armour was in widespread use and was as mobile as possible while offering excellent protection. Each piece of the armour had a specific name and function. Plate armour of this sort distributed weight better than a hauberk and was not very restrictive, though it was heavy and tiring to wear. Stories of knights winched onto their horses are mostly myths. Younger knights would at times perform gymnastics in their armour.

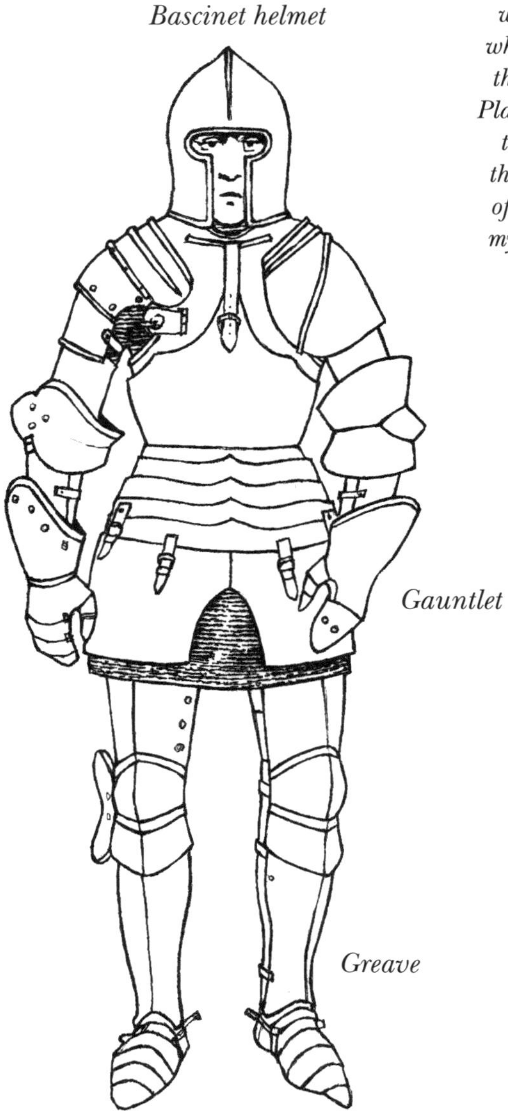

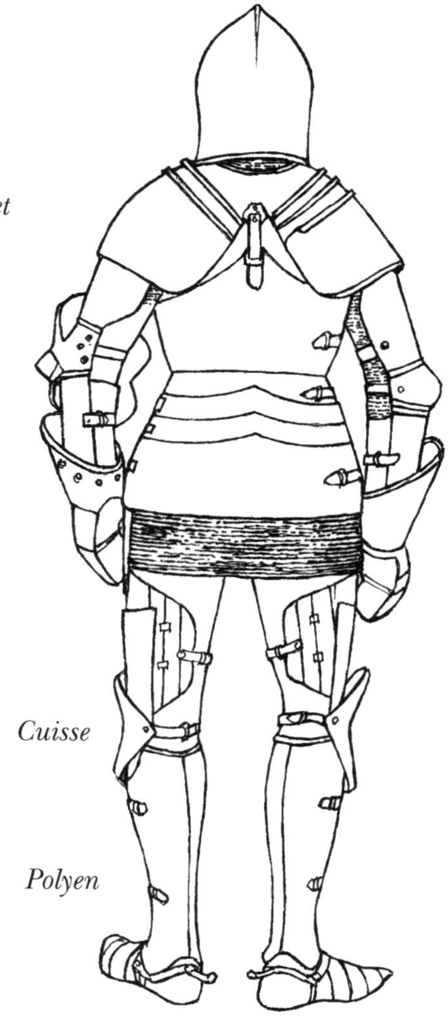

Armouring the Limbs

The long surfaces of the limbs are relatively easy to cover in armour, but the joints pose serious problems. Mail is always an option but as with other parts of the body articulated plates, assisted by mail, provided a better set of options. Chain mail trews were referred to as chausses, which could also mean conventional leg coverings. Whether the term meant clothing or armour would normally be clear from the context. Chausses could be reinforced with plate shin protectors known as schynbalds. Feet might be protected by stout leather boots or by articulated sabaton. Some designs of sabaton were optimized for use on horseback and made it virtually impossible to walk on foot.

Knee and foot protection were important not only to defend against an enemy's weapons. Horses might collide in a charge or melee, possibly crushing the rider's foot or leg. A shield, driven down by a powerful blow, could cause a secondary injury. The armour itself could be a liability if damaged: dented lames might jam, limiting mobility on foot even though there was no injury.

Knees are particularly vulnerable to blunt force attacks but require a large range of motion. This problem was solved by the poleyn, an articulated knee covering that might extend as much as halfway up the thigh and down the shin. The poleyn appeared in the early 1200s as a reinforcement for chain armour or could be worn independently, with only trousers and boots protecting the rest of the leg.

Additional or improved protection for the upper and lower legs was provided by cuisses and greaves respectively, which might be worn

This protection for the neck and shoulders is the most complete example known of one the rarest forms of iron lamellar armour from Tibet (15th century). Lamellar armour is characterized by upwardly overlapping rows of small, finger-sized plates, in which the individual lamellae, and the rows they create, are joined together by an intricate system of leather lacing, requiring no other internal support fabric or lining for its structure or functionality.

over mail or instead of it. As armour technology advanced, leg protection developed from a set of separate pieces into a single integrated leg protector covering the thigh, shin and knee, and often including armour for the foot as well.

Arms were protected in a similar way, with the couter evolving a simple curved metal plate shielding the elbow joint into an articulated piece protecting more of the arm. The upper arm and shoulder were covered by a rerebrace and gardbrace respectively, with a vambrace on the forearm. As with leg armour, these pieces developed over time and were combined to create a complete system of arm protection.

Dating from 1590, these armour pieces combine cuisses to protect the thighs with articulated poleyns for the knees, allowing coverage without restricting movement.

The vambrace protects the forearm, while the coulter shields the elbow. These Italian examples date from around 1450.

GAUNTLET

The hands are an obvious weak point in any armour system. While flexible protection like mail can stop a blow, the small bones of the hand and fingers are easily broken. In mounted combat, deliberately targeting the hands is extremely difficult, but a warrior must extend them to wield a weapon, exposing them to accidental injury. On foot, targeting an opponent's hands was a key focus in combat training, as fingers could be lost or hands crushed during battle.

Gloves reinforced with mail or metal splints provided some protection but still had numerous vulnerable points – what modern users of protective gear sometimes call 'Murphy spots'. Murphy's Law of Armour suggests that 'any attack that lands, will land in the worst possible place'. Even a sword tip caught between the fingers could incapacitate the best-trained knight, often permanently.

Plate gauntlets can be divided into two general types. Mitten gauntlets offer the greatest protection but provide little dexterity. They consist of articulated lames big enough to spread an impact out over the whole hand and strong enough to resist a considerable blow. They are also more likely to deflect a weapon than fingered gauntlets, which are more dextrous but provide less protection.

Above: Left arm vambrace (Italian, ca. 1380–1400). This vambrace is one of the few pieces that have survived with their original brass borders intact.

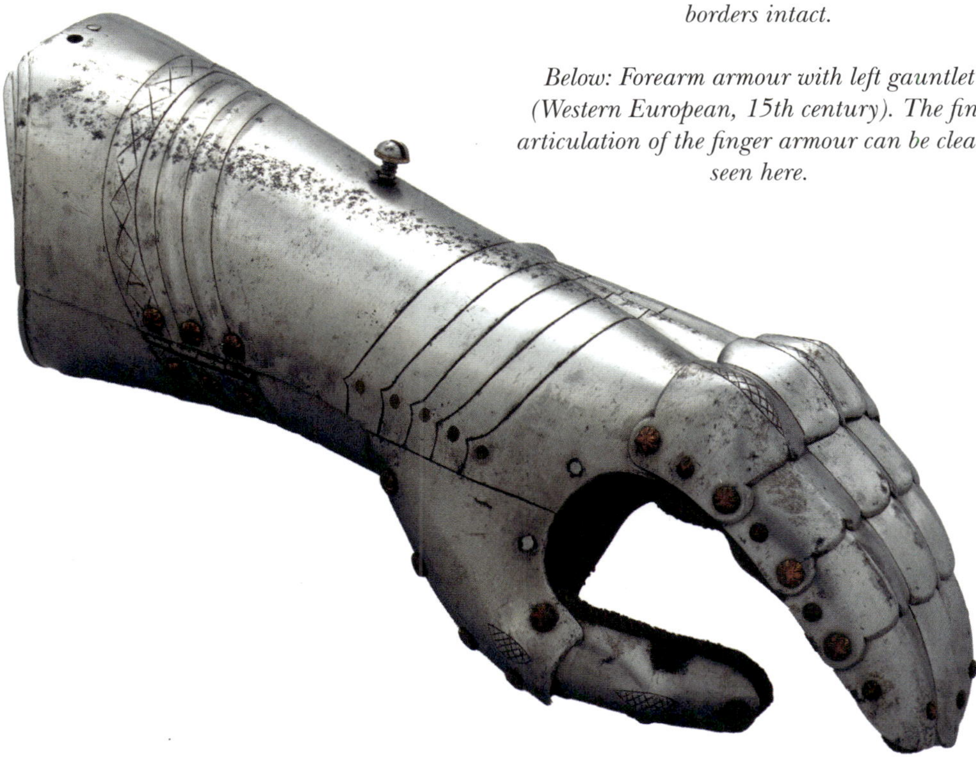

Below: Forearm armour with left gauntlet (Western European, 15th century). The fine articulation of the finger armour can be clearly seen here.

Duelling gauntlets produced in Nuremberg, Germany, dating to around 1560 to 1610. The right palm has no mail, to facilitate holding the sword, while the left palm is protected since grabbing an opponent's blade was a recognized tactic at the time.

Lefthand gauntlet, Italian, 1450. The gauntlet consists of a single plate of metal, providing protection but more limited movement. This is part of a large find of medieval armour discovered in 1840 in the ruins of the fortress of Chalcis, on the Greek island of Euboea.

Highly decorated mitten-type gauntlets made in Germany around 1535. Protection extends over the wrist and lower part of the forearm.

The wrist is another vulnerable area. The forearm bones can be easily broken, tendons operating the hand can be cut, and a major artery runs along the inner wrist. Cuts to the forearm were extremely common in sword combat, much like injuries to the fingers and hands. Consequently, armoured gauntlets needed to overlap or at least abut the forearm protection to ensure continuous coverage.

From Mail Coat to Full Harness

An early medieval warrior wearing a mail coat and an open-faced helm with a nasal bar had an enormous advantage over an unarmoured opponent, yet remained vulnerable to many common weapons.

The Battle of Roosebeke on 27 November 1382 (miniature from the Grandes Chroniques de France *by Jean Froissart, ca 1470–75). Despite the Flemish army deploying cannon (left), the French heavy cavalry (right) broke the tightly packed Flemish ranks, leading to a massive rout where many died by trampling or suffocation.*

He would have fought with spear and shield, whether on foot or horseback, using a sword or possibly an axe as a secondary weapon. His opponents wielded similar arms, which could still be effective against his armour.

His counterpart in the Late Medieval period was almost invulnerable to the same weapons, providing he kept moving. The horse served not just as transport or an attack platform: it was also a vital element of the knight's survival. An armoured warrior on foot could be dragged to the ground or restrained by a determined opponent, whereas a knight on horseback could often force his way free, even when surrounded.

It was no coincidence that wrestling was included in a knight's training. Beyond fostering martial spirit and physical fitness, wrestling taught skills essential for breaking free from an opponent or bringing one down for a killing stroke. As combatants grew tired, their blows weakened and became less accurate, reducing the likelihood of delivering a disabling hit. As a result, fighting techniques evolved that used weapons as grappling tools, for hooking or tripping an opponent.

Infantry weapons naturally evolved to deal with increasingly heavy armour. Complex pole weapons typically incorporated a spearhead and a hammer or pick, as well as a hook that could be used to drag a horseman off his mount. A swing with the hammer or a thrust with the

Opposite: A two-handed sword dating from 1400–50. The development and use of such weapons was both enabled and driven by armour protection strong enough that a shield was no longer a necessary part of a warrior's equipment.

spearpoint was almost certain to be defeated by plate armour if made while the horseman was mobile. A downed knight, on the other hand, was vulnerable to blunt force strokes battering through his armour or a downward thrust with a second spike on the opposite end of a pole weapon. If held down, he could be finished off with a thin-bladed knife inserted through the armpits, eye slits or groin.

The improved efficiency of armour further widened the 'survival gap' between knights and ordinary foot soldiers. Even as firearms became more powerful, those who could afford good quality armour were far less likely to be injured by a common soldier. Certain weapons, notably the English longbow, could penetrate armour but required years

The pollaxe provided several ways to attack an armoured opponent. It could be used to stab, hack, or hook a knight to unseat him from his horse. Pollaxe fighting became a central feature of late medieval tourneys, often governed by rules specifying the exact design of the weapon to be used.

of training and the development of specialist muscle to use effectively. Essentially, combat effectiveness against the armoured knight was the province of those able to obtain both the equipment and the training necessary to stand against them.

One consequence of this was the use of two-handed weapons on foot, replacing the traditional combination of hand weapon and shield. In this context, a good defence contributed to improved offensive capability, which once again advantaged those who had effective armour and those who did not.

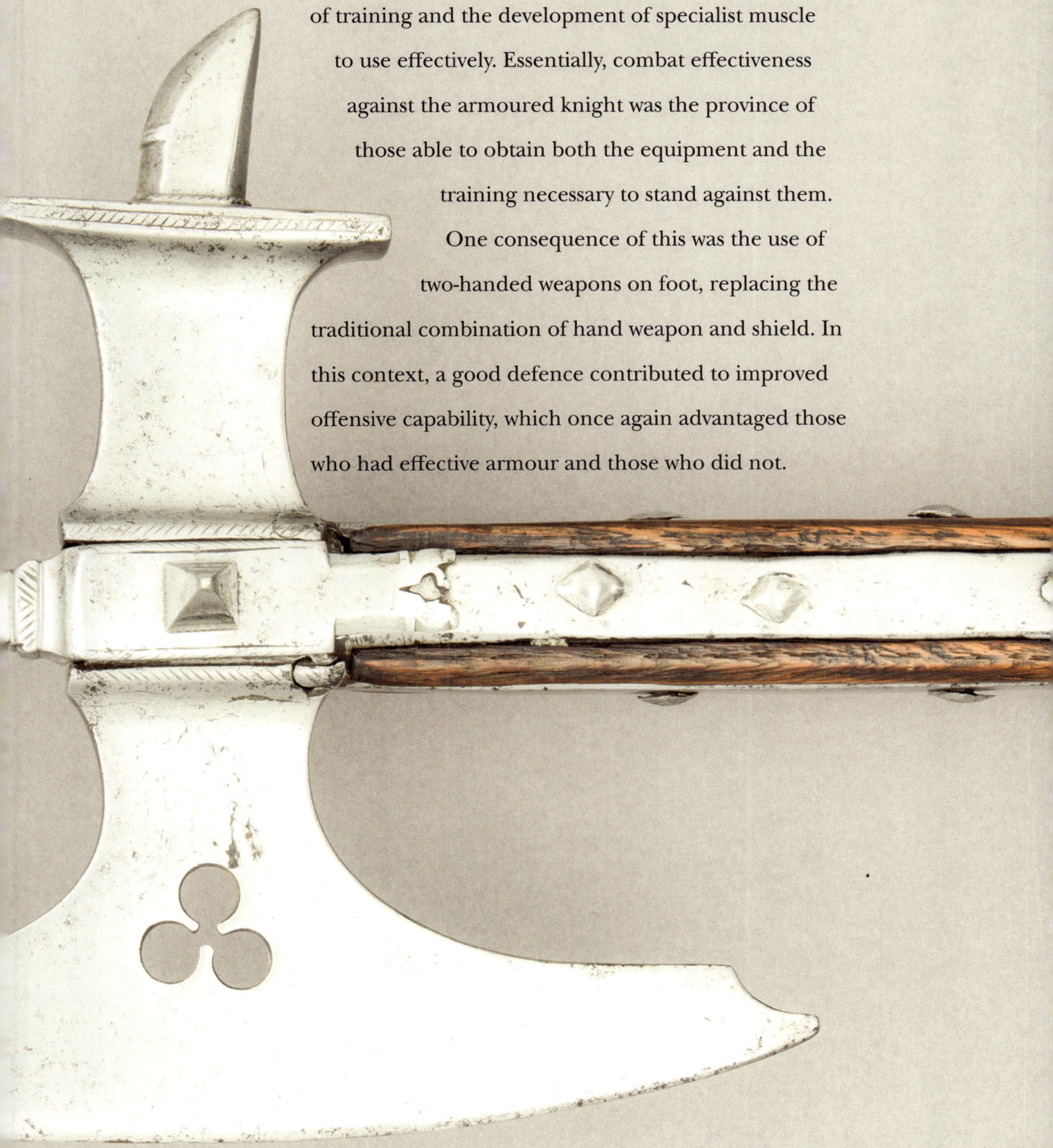

Much of our knowledge of medieval fighting techniques comes from fechtbuchs *(fencing manuals) written by masters like Hans Talhoffer. Wrestling was not only used for training and fitness, but was also a vital skill for confronting near-invulnerable armoured opponents.*

Vß dem ryglins fassen. So zuckt
Er den andern arm. vnd ergrifft
In by dem hopt. vnd verwirfft
In von Im

Robert Radcliffe, Earl of Sussex (1483–1542), served kings Henry VII and Henry VIII of England. He is depicted here wearing pauldrons (shoulder armour), metal cuirass and gauntlets, all key elements of the medieval knight's armour.

CHAPTER 4

The Armoured Knight

THE ARMOURED KNIGHT was a formidable fighting force throughout the medieval era, although the popular image of full plate armour adorned with heraldic symbols on the shield only emerged in later years. The knight was very much a product of his period, in many ways reflecting the culture, politics and technological capabilities of the time.

Knights, and the nobility in general, are closely associated with the sword. In some regions, laws even prohibited non-nobles from owning one. Workarounds existed, however. The German *grosse messer*, literally a 'big knife', resembles a sword and can be wielded like one, but its construction classifies it as a knife rather than a sword, making it legal for a peasant to possess.

The sword proper was a symbol of authority as well as a sidearm. It was relatively convenient to carry and effective enough against most opponents. The sword would not be the first choice of an armoured knight going into battle, however. He would prefer to fight with a spear or lance, and might switch to a hammer or axe for close combat.

The fighters shown in this 15th century image from the Jagiellonian Library in Krakow are armed with sword-like messers and a spiked Hungarian shield that worked much like a buckler, with the additional capability to stab an opponent.

All of these weapons are objectively more effective than swords when used in massed combat. Yet it was the sword that symbolized knighthood and served as the instrument by which it was conferred. Early in the period, any knight could elevate someone to the same status, with as much or as little ceremony as he thought proper. One common factor was the new knight receiving his status by way of a touch on the shoulder with the flat of a sword blade.

With so little regulation, it might seem strange that more people were not knighted, perhaps in return for money or favours. However, there were reasons why a knight would not go around ennobling others at random. One was jealousy of his own status. If the kingdom had vast numbers of dubious knights, the value of the status was diminished. Even if the knight himself did not care, others would – and they were well-equipped men of war. There was also a measure of responsibility and the maintenance of standards. A knight had to be trained and equipped in order to fulfil his function, and someone who recklessly knighted people who could not afford the equipment or perform the required service would wreck his own reputation.

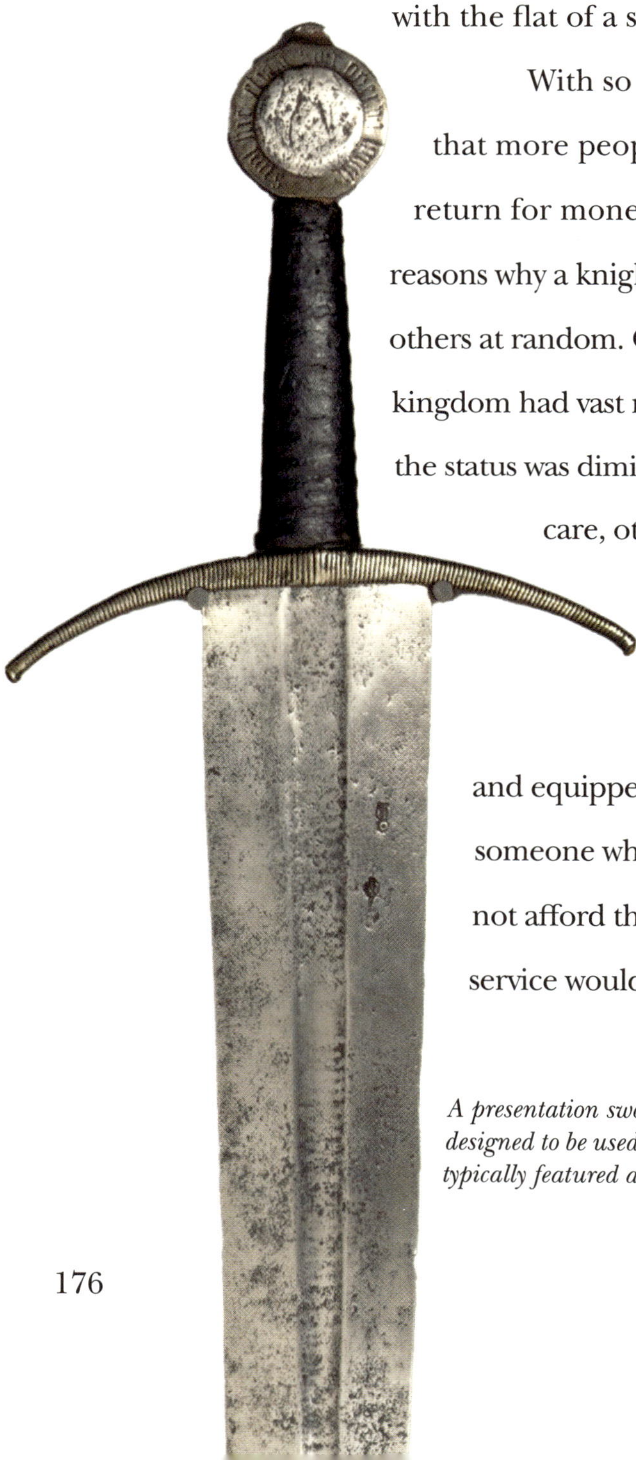

A presentation sword dating from around 1400. Swords of this era were designed to be used alongside armour that included hand protection, and typically featured a very basic hilt.

By the 14th century, multiple variants on the arming sword – the knight's signature weapon – had emerged. The spada da stocco *(far right) was developed to counter heavy armour, focusing on thrusting attacks aimed at weak points.*

Standards varied from place to place, but a knight was expected to own and be able to maintain a warhorse, full armour and suitable weapons. He might be supported by his lord or granted an estate to provide an income, but either way maintaining a force of knights was expensive. The return on this investment was a duty on the part of the knight to perform military service.

This could involve little more than attending his lord's court as both a status symbol and a personal bodyguard, or it could entail travelling across the Mediterranean to follow the lord on a crusade.

Chivalry

The concept of chivalry evolved over time and varied regionally. It was heavily influenced by Christian virtues such as piety and humility, and derived from the clear expectations placed upon a warrior in service to a social superior. Knights were expected to be loyal to their lord and to have sufficient skill at arms to be worth supporting. They were expected to face their enemies and fight bravely. In short, a knight needed to be a military and security asset: dependable and effective.

These fundamental values were reinforced by social expectations. A chivalrous knight was expected to be generous and unconcerned with worldly riches, respectful towards women and kind to the poor. He was expected to act fairly in both his dealings and in his battles, and to remain a devout Christian. The importance placed on these virtues, however, could vary considerably. In some cases, these requirements applied only to a segment of society. For example, the chivalrous knight

A German depiction of a knight on horseback, dating from around 1520.

was expected to respect noble women and to be kind to social equals but could do what he liked to the lower orders without a stain on his honour. The requirement to fight fairly applied only to fellow knights; peasants could take their chances.

TOURNEY ARMOUR

Some knights owned entirely separate sets of battle and tournament armour, while others had a single suit that could carry extra plates for tournament use. Tourney armour was characterized by being much stronger on the knight's left side, where a lance would impact. Outer plates augmented the arm protection and breastplate, and there was often a neck guard to deflect a blow away from the neck and throat. Tournament armour was the top-end designer sportswear of its day, and was decorated accordingly. It was common to decorate helms with figurines of real or mythological creatures, sometimes connected with the knights arms. The knight depicted here has a unicorn on his helm and shield.

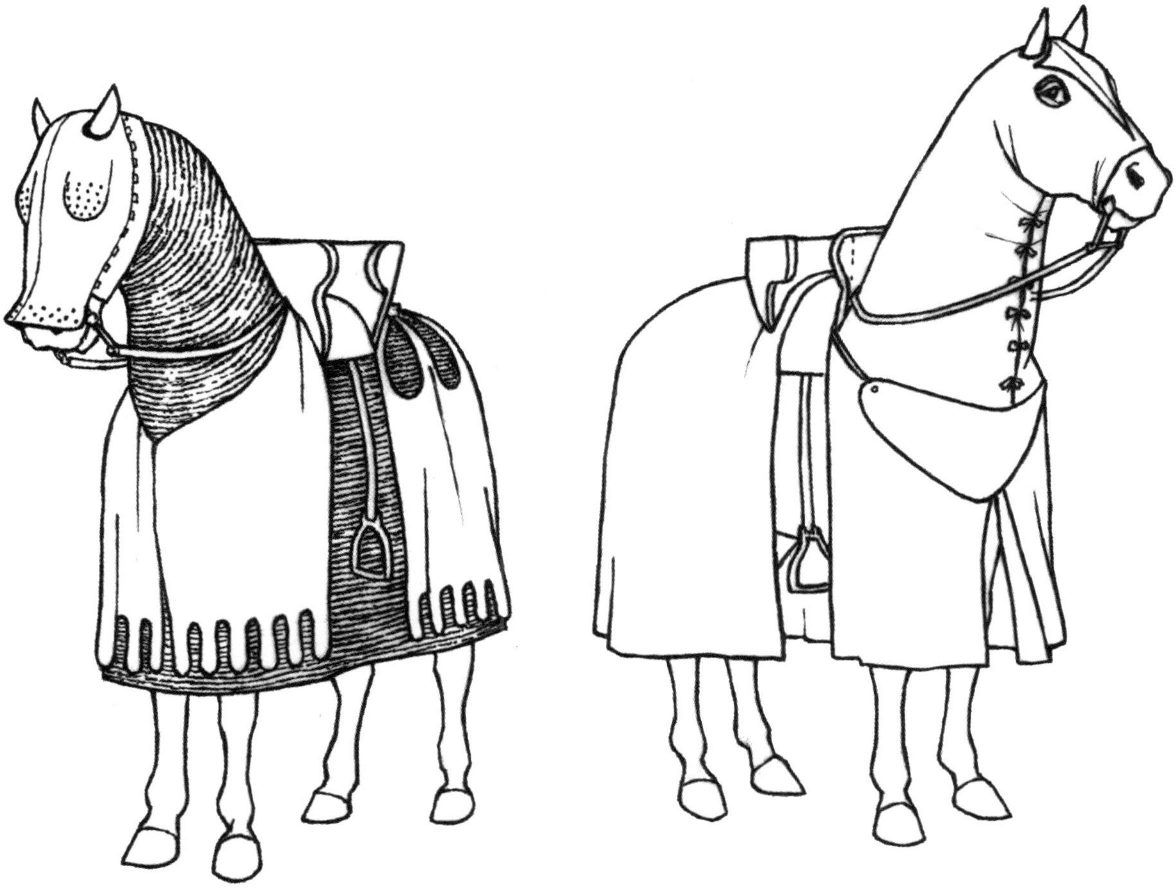

Horse protection at its most basic took the form of a thick blanket that might cushion a blow but was mainly useful because it could entangle weapons and prevent a solid contact. However, this was no use against arrows so gradually horses gained leather or metal armour. The head, neck and flanks of a horse were most likely hit by blows with hand weapons, and could be protected relatively easily. Plunging arrows, on the other hand, were likely to strike the animal's back, which was more difficult to protect to a degree that would prevent the arrow penetrating. The massed volleys of English longbowmen could unhorse knights and kill their mounts from beyond the range where the knights could reply.

King Charles V of France presenting the sword of Constable of France to Bertrand du Guesclin, circa 1415. Bertrand du Guesclin was a Breton knight and French military commander during the Hundred Years' War. From Grandes Chroniques de France.

A 15th century model of an armoured warrior on horseback from the Musee de l'Armee Dome des Invalides in Paris. The horse is equipped with armour protection for its head and face, known as a chanfron.

An example of Gothic armour. The armour of the late fifteenth century was elegant as well as functional, offering excellent protection and very little restriction of mobility. Advances in metallurgy meant that thinner plates could provide a level of protection previously afforded only by clumsy and heavy armour. The main piece was the breastplate, with chainmail protecting the groin, armpits and other areas where plates were not appropriate. The front of the saddle provided extra cover for the rider's groin. The arms and shoulders were protected by articulated plates and from downward blows by the flared rim of the helm.

At the battle of Poitiers in 1356, King John of France signalled his surrender to the English Earl of Warwick by removing his armoured gantlet, symbolically placing himself at the nobleman's mercy.

This applied even more so to the non-Christian societies of Europe. Crusaders in the Holy Land, supposedly campaigning in the name of God, committed terrible atrocities against non-Christians. Among these were incidents of civilians in a captured city being cut open to see if they had hidden their valuables by swallowing them.

The illustration is from the 16th century Album of Tournaments and Parades in Nuremberg, *specifically showing knights prepared for a joust. Elaborate crests mounted atop the helm, together with brightly coloured accoutrements, added to the spectacle of the tournament and made participants easily identifiable to spectators. Such display was not merely decorative; it was a deliberate expression of wealth, status and power – much like the pageantry of a modern military parade.*

Despite its failures, the code of chivalry did temper the violent character of the knightly class. The existence of a formal code meant that there was a standard to judge a knight against or to compare him to. Peer pressure might restrain the worst excesses of those of bad character, and the code permitted a more permanent form of social correction.

A young knight wanting to make a name for himself had multiple excuses to challenge someone who was not following the code. He might or might not care about cruelty towards the common folk but protecting the weak was a suitable pretext for issuing a challenge. Allegations of disloyalty or treachery were extremely serious and likely to result in a challenge.

Although it led to individual acts of violence, this situation had the overall effect of making society more stable and peaceful. Those who strayed too far from the ideal of a 'gentle knight' who knew his place in the social order and did not allow himself to be ruled by greed would find themselves the subject of challenges from young hotheads – and perhaps also those who genuinely wanted to punish their wrongdoing.

The Tourney

Originally, a tourney was an informal – or perhaps totally unplanned – meeting between a small number of knights who would then test their skills against one another. This was a rather hazardous business as live

Opposite: By the 15th century, the tourney consisted of multiple distinct events. Jousting with lances remained popular but entertainment also included individual combat on foot, group fights and a grand melee in which knights could capture others and earn a ransom.

TOURNEY CHAMPION: THE YOUNG KING

Tourneys also helped remind the common folk about the power of their overlords. Witnessing their lord's knights in action was a stark reminder that those who objected to paying their taxes would have to face them. On the reverse side of that coin, a good tourney entertained the people and created heroes for them. One such hero was the second son of Henry II of England by Eleanor of Aquitaine.

Known as Henry the Young King, Henry was the older brother of Richard I and John, and would probably have succeeded his father before them had he lived. In 1175 he embarked on a tour of the tourneys of France where he won tremendous honour and glory. Henry the Young King was the equivalent of a modern rock star or top athlete, but he died of dysentery in 1183 aged 28.

weapons were used. Casualties were inevitable but armour protection was effective enough to keep the death toll to an acceptable level.

Although rather brutal, informal tourneys of this kind ensured the warrior class did not neglect their training. A social code that vilified anyone who refused a challenge from a social equal meant that knights might have to fight at any time and created a form of natural selection among the warrior elite. Many tales tell of knights waiting at a bridge or similar crossing and challenging all who wished to pass. While such scenes belong largely to the realm of adventure fiction, they reflect a real

Opposite: This is a German post-medieval tilting-style armour, likely created by Anton Peffenhauser around 1575.

practice: the 'informal tourney', in which knights might joust with those they met or actively seek out worthy opponents to test their skills.

The joust in this context was a term for any encounter, on foot or horseback, but over time it came to refer to mounted combat with the lance. The tourney, too, became a more organized affair with prizes for the winners in several categories. These ran the full

COUCHED LANCE

The couched lance, held cradled under the arm and directed more or less straight ahead, was in use even before the invention of the stirrup. Stirrups, however, allowed the rider to absorb far greater impact without being unseated. Some jousts were competitions of technical skill, where the aim was to break a lance on the opponent's shield, but for much of the period the aim was to simply knock the opponent clean off his mount. The force generated in a mutual lance charge, even with blunt weapons, was enormous, leading to the development of specialized tourney armour. This reinforced the likely impact points and could be heavier than battle armour as the wearer was active only for short periods.

Jousting armour could be tailored specially for lance combat, unlike general-purpose armour. Not only were the likely impact points predictable, enabling thickening and shaping of the armour, but it did not matter if mobility was limited outside the actions of the lance. Armour that restricted the ability to use a sword or other hand weapon would be a liability in battle, but could be an asset in a tourney.

spectrum of knightly endeavour, including mounted combat, fighting on foot and wrestling.

The tourney was a training or proving ground, but its significance extended beyond that. An extravagant tourney allowed a lord to show off his wealth and the prowess of his fighting men, which could be useful in both internal and external politics. Those who sought advancement might attract the attention of powerful people, and a glorious tournament with many feats of arms was a bold political statement aimed at potential enemies. There were other prizes to be won in the tourney. A lady might show her favour for a knight by granting

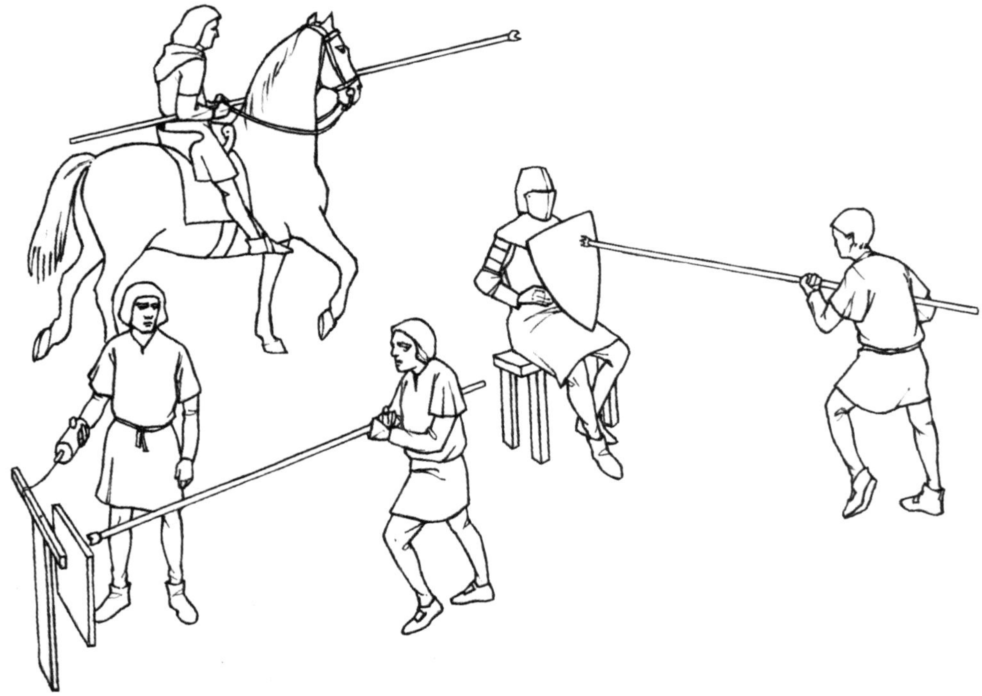

Squires and young knights learned to ride a warhorse and to handle the lance separately before they tried to do both at once. Among the challenges they faced were the quintain, a revolving post with a target and a weight on its arms and trying to knock an armoured knight off his stool by charging at him with a lance. Once a suitable level of skill had been acquired the young knight could try his luck against a full-sized quintain on horseback.

An image from the Tournament Book *of René d'Anjou (1447). Tourneys were a riot of colour and noise. At their core, they demonstrated the power and martial prowess of the knightly class, with their expensive armour on display.*

him a token to display in the tourney, perhaps leading to a romance or political marriage.

The tourney reached its peak with an event known as the Field of the Cloth of Gold, in 1520. This was a tremendous spectacle but also a political meeting between Henry VIII of England and Francis I of France. Both monarchs likely hoped the feats of arms performed by their knights would intimidate the other side and make negotiations easier. In the end, however, the political results were minimal.

Weapons of the Medieval Knight

As previously noted the medieval knight was primarily associated with the sword as a sidearm and symbol of authority. The long-bladed sword was a developed technology in the Early Medieval period, consisting of a double-edged cutting blade with a point suitable for thrusting, a handgrip and sometimes a form of hand protection.

Terminology for specific types of swords is often debated, and in many cases the labels were applied centuries after the weapons were in use. Even within general types there is considerable variation. Some weapons had a double or single fuller – a groove along the blade where material had been removed. This was to reduce weight without weakening the blade, and had nothing to do with allowing the opponent's blood to escape so as to prevent the weapon becoming stuck. Nevertheless, the

Opposite: Field armour of King Henry VIII of England. In his youth Henry was renowned as a great tournament fighter, but paid the price. The unhealed wound that plagued him in later life stemmed from a jousting injury received in 1536.

Trial by combat was – officially, at least – meant to determine the right in a dispute through divine judgement. In practice, however, the advantage lay with the richer combatant, who could afford superior armour and thus better withstand an opponent's blows.

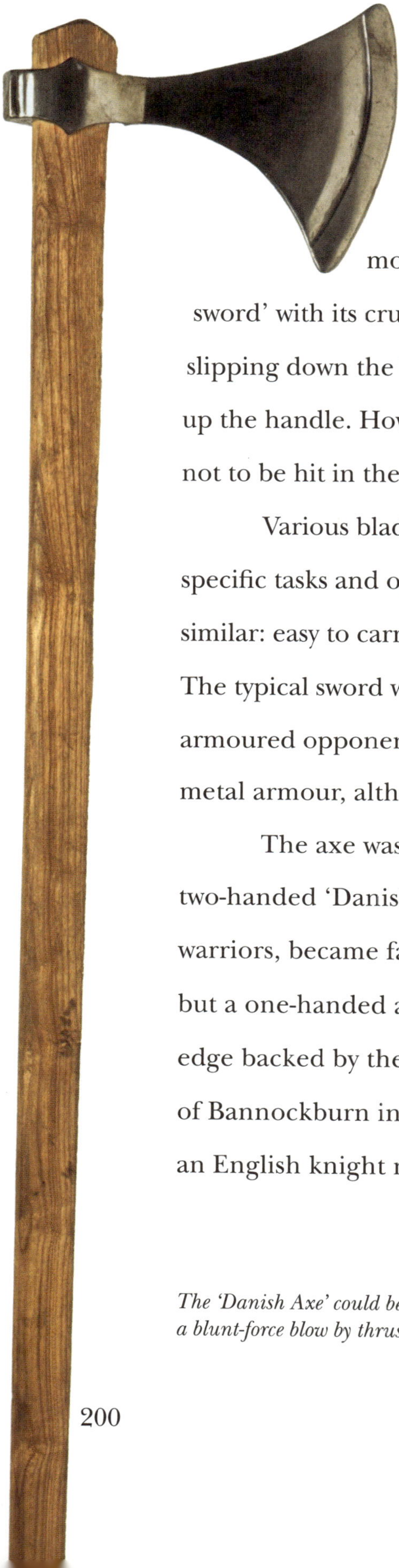

myth of the 'blood gutter' remains common.

The so-called 'Viking sword' of the Early Medieval period was intended for use with a shield and had minimal hand protection. It gradually morphed into the classic 'knightly sword' or 'arming sword' with its cruciform hilt, which prevented the user's hand from slipping down the blade and blocked an opponent's weapon from sliding up the handle. However good the wielder's gauntlets were, it was better not to be hit in the hand.

Various blade and handle lengths tailored the knight's sword to specific tasks and opponents, but its overall characteristics remained similar: easy to carry compared to many other weapons and versatile. The typical sword was effective mainly against unarmoured and lightly armoured opponents. Its slicing action was defeated with relative ease by metal armour, although a thrust at a weak point would be effective.

The axe was a potent weapon on horseback or on foot. The two-handed 'Danish Axe', favoured by many Norse and Anglo-Saxon warriors, became far less common once horsed combat was the norm, but a one-handed axe could deliver a fearsome blow with the sharp edge backed by the concentrated weight of the weapon. At the Battle of Bannockburn in 1314, Scottish king Robert the Bruce encountered an English knight named Henry de Bohun. De Bohun's helm – and

The 'Danish Axe' could be used to hook an opponent's shield and pull him off balance, or to deliver a blunt-force blow by thrusting over the shield.

his head inside – were cloven by Robert the Bruce's axe, although the weapon broke in the clash.

Daggers were also useful in despatching a grappled or downed opponent. Medieval *fechtbuchs* (fighting manuals) often include extensive sections on using a weapon such as a rondel dagger. These were stiff-bladed stabbing knives intended to find the gaps in an opponent's armour. The development of knightly weapons – and those of the common infantryman – was directed by the improvement of armour protection and vice versa. Lack of armour also caused a change in weapon design. The social upheaval caused by the Black Death resulted in the rise of a new, monied middle class who naturally wanted swords as status symbols and for self-defence.

Robert the Bruce defeats the armour of Sir Henry Bohun by hitting him so hard the haft of Robert's axe breaks.

Left & right: French and English rondel daggers were intended to defeat armour by a close-quarters thrust into a weak spot, delivered after the opponent had been wrestled into a vulnerable position.

Opposite: The knight's arming sword gradually gained hand protection, evolving into the espada ropera, *or 'sword of the cloth' – a weapon intended for use when not wearing armour. The name has since been Anglicized as 'rapier'.*

Early tournaments were fought with the knight's normal battle gear, but as the period advanced specialist tournament gear became available for those who could afford it. Tournament armour was too heavy and restrictive for battle use, but provided extra protection against the repeated lance impacts of the joust. Extra plates were added, to prevent a lance point finding the user's armpit or neck, both of which could be fatal. Face protection was also crucial. Henry II of France was mortally wounded in 1559 during a joust, when a splinter of a broken lance penetrated his eye. The helm was shaped to deflect blows as much as possible.

The knightly arming sword gradually morphed into the *espada ropera*, or 'sword of the cloth'. Known in English as the rapier, this weapon developed increasingly elaborate hand protection which, in the hands of a skilled user, also helped protect the head and body.

Sword use diverged after the medieval period. In military contexts, swords were generally used in partial armour. Civilian users had to rely solely on their weapon for protection. This gave rise to the Art of Defence, or fencing, whereby the user's skill replaced armour. Perhaps not coincidentally, the fencing master's *salle* also became a social place where gentlemen made useful acquaintances and impressed their peers with their skill.

THE LANCE

The lance, sometimes used on foot as a spear, was capable of penetrating much of the armour of the day. Driven home with all the force of a charging horse, it might punch through quite thick armour, and even on foot the flexing of the haft could provide a springing action that drove the point forward and magnified the user's strength. A spear thrust might be deflected by armour but there was always the chance the point would skid until it found a 'blade trap' such as the neck, armpit or groin. These areas were designed so that a weapon's point could catch, and they were notoriously hard to armour.

BLUNT WEAPONS

The mace amplified the concept of blunt force trauma to its extreme. Whether flanged or not, it could dent plate armour severely enough to hinder movement or breathing, while also breaking bones or causing concussions. While anything but subtle or elegant, a mace was a better option than a typical sword against the armour of the Late Medieval period. Flails, consisting of a solid or spiked head connected to a haft by a length of cord or chain, could deliver a tremendous blow but were not popular weapons for the nobility. Blind King John of Bohemia is a notable exception. It is said that he 'flailed about' to considerable effect at the Battle of Crécy before being killed. The war hammer or pick was designed to punch through armour, combining heavy impact with a semi-sharp point. One-handed versions for use with a shield or on horseback became popular as plate armour developed in this period, and the effectiveness of that armour against most weapons allowed knights to make use of a two-handed version.

Weapons of this type usually had a combination head, with a hammer on one side and a pointed pick on the other. A spike, of varying length, offered the capability to make a thrust in the manner of a spear. While bashing at the opponent could certainly be effective, much depended on where the blow landed and how squarely. Battering an opponent into submission was a tiring business, but a skilled knight could trip his opponent or perhaps wrestle him to the ground where he would be far more vulnerable.

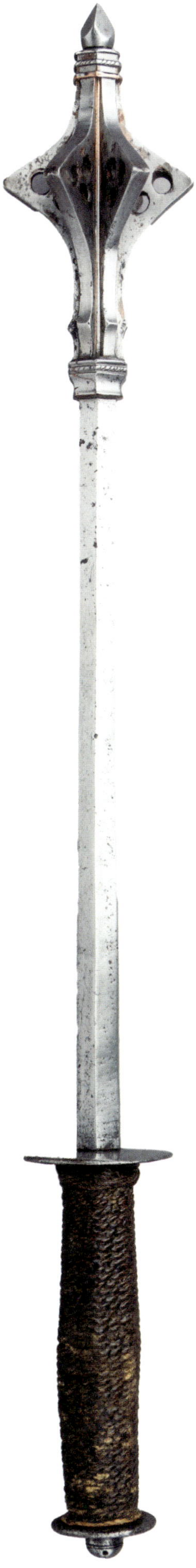

The arms race between armour and weaponry resulted in specialist weapons like this German mace from 1480–1500 (left) and French war hammer of 1450 (right). Concentration of force at a single point represented the only reliable way to get through the armour of the day.

The Brandes family, originating in Bavaria, adopted a crest displaying seven bees (left), whereas the Hirschman family, probably from Silesia, chose a deer as their main emblem (right). Variations on these designs were used to distinguish between brothers and sons in the same lineage.

CHAPTER 5

Heraldry

THE CONCEPTS underlying formal heraldry date back to ancient times, when warriors decorated their shields with tribal, religious or personal images. The move towards a formal system of heraldry began in the 1100s, and is widely thought to have been driven by the use of full-face helms that made it difficult to identify friend or foe on the battlefield. This is questionable, however, in that it assumes warriors would previously have been able to identify their allies through facial recognition in the midst of a chaotic battlefield.

Morale Booster

Some knights and lords had a sufficiently fearsome reputation that their presence on the field might reduce enemy morale. The opposite was also true: leadership in those times was heroic, so knowing their side's champions and leaders were still in the fight was important. A tired and heavily besieged knight would be reassured by seeing the heraldic device of a friend or lord remaining engaged, and might be disheartened to the point of fleeing if he thought his king had fled.

The identification function of heraldic devices could be fulfilled by a less formal system of symbols, but over time a standardized set of

Portuguese and Castilian knights fighting with spears, morning stars and two-handed axes at the at the Battle of Aljubarrota, 1385. In this significant battle, the forces of King John I of Portugal defeated those of King John I of Castile, securing independence for the Portuguese kingdom. The coat of arms of Castile are displayed prominently, featuring yellow castles on red and a lion on white. From Chronique d' Angleterre *(15th century).*

This heraldic device from 12th-century France appears on a sword pommel, indicating the noble family the bearer served. No records survive identifying which family used this emblem, however.

devices emerged, along with rules for using them. Specific arrangements of symbols, as well as certain symbols themselves, became the property of noble families, representing the family's history and circumstances.

The earliest known record of heraldry as we know it today is the gift of a shield to Geoffrey, Count of Anjou in 1127 from his father Henry I of England. By the end of the century heraldry had become prevalent throughout Europe. There were initially no formal rules for what devices could be used and by whom, although it was customary for an eldest son to use his father's device. It was not until 1484 that a formal College of Arms was founded in England to regulate the use of heraldic symbols. Codifying the arms of all noble families required an undertaking known as the Visitations, in which the heralds met with nobles and recorded the symbols they were using.

Heraldic Conventions

A system of what colours and devices could be used gradually emerged from the chaotic free-for-all, along with standard versions of the symbology and specific names describing them. The face of a shield, upon which heradic devices were displayed, was known as the field. The field could be left plain or divided into sections to hold multiple

Geoffrey of Anjou married Matilda, the daughter of King Henry I of England, thereby founding the powerful Plantagenet dynasty. He is famously associated with an early example of heraldry featuring six golden lions on a blue background, shown here on his shield.

Heraldic devices were displayed on shields and clothing, enabling the quick identification of prominent people – such as the Duke of Normandy depicted here (1380–1422). This was as important in courtly or ceremonial settings as it was on the battlefield.

elements. When the field was divided, the pattern of division had a specific name, and the resulting shapes were known as ordinaries.

A field divided vertically was per pale while a horizontal division was per fess. A diagonal subdivision was per bend, or per bend sinister if reversed. A triangular subdivision was per chevron. A bar across the top of the shield was per chief and a diagonal line was per bend. A field could also be divided into four quarters horizontally and vertically (per cross) or diagonally (per saltire). Other, more complex subdivisions were possible, each with its own specific name.

Colours

The main divisions of the shield were coloured using a specific palette subdivided into colours and 'metals'. The fundamental rule was that a coloured object should not be placed on a coloured background, nor metals applied on a background of other metals. This created a striking visual contrast, forming the first impression a viewer would have of the bearer's arms.

The five traditional colours were gules (red), azure (blue), vert (green), sable (black) and purpure (purple), which could be combined with the two metals: argent (silver/white) and or (gold/yellow). Two additional colour schemes were known as furs: ermine (white and black) and vair (blue and white). Some objects, notably creatures, could be depicted in their natural colouration, known as proper, and could be placed on a coloured or metal field. The same applied to furs. Greater complexity was possible by the use of additional shapes within a design,

per fess ermine and vert

per pale and azure

per bend argent and azure

per chevron and gules

per saltire argent and gules

gyronny and sable

Above: While confusing to outsiders, the specialist terminology of heraldry provides a standardized format to accurately describe the elements used and their relation to one another.

Opposite: Four cavaliers depicted in the 15th century Libro de los Caballeros de la Cofradia de Santiago *(*Book of the Knights of the Brotherhood of Santiago*), the oldest surviving equestrian armorial.*

known as subordinaries, and by various designs of dividing lines. In addition, a shield might bear one or more charges. Some of these were simple geometric shapes such as diamonds, rings and stars, some more complex designs such as flowers, and others depicted animals.

Each animal symbolized a virtue such as courage or loyalty, and was depicted in one of several standard poses. An animal depicted standing naturally was standant; one rearing up was rampant. A walking creature was passant, and one looking at the viewer was gardant.

Regidor
Pero Ruyz de villegas
Regidor
Pedro de arçeo
Regidor

... emus / se toti exercitio
armoru[m] / tradidit / et quod / tande[m] / ornat[us] est militari
Cingulo / et in eo exercitio / mortuus / sepult[us] est Verone
i[n] maiori ecclesia Hec latius legunt[ur] i[n] cronicis
que sunt apud d. Jacobu[m] de fabris . cive[m] Veronesem
et Egregiu[m] Juris Utriusq[ue] doctore[m] Et in
annalib[us] compilatis a Johan[n]e de Radic[ibus]
patavo .

Complex designs could be created using these elements, and the situation was further complicated when a device passed to the next generation.

Coat of Arms

A system of cadency marks, applied to the chief (upper part) of the shield, indicated which son the arms belonged to. When the eldest son inherited his father's position, his cadency mark was removed – he used the crest of the family he now led. For younger sons their cadency mark was included in future iterations of their arms, enabling those who knew the system to trace their lineage.

Above: Heraldry, as a means of identifying friend or foe, was less important when fighting enemies such as the Saracens, whose equipment and appearance were markedly different from those of the Crusaders. Nonetheless, it was still important for locating leaders on the battlefield.

Opposite: A Veronese knight of the early 15th century as depicted in the Codex Capodilista.

PENNON

Arms were not only displayed on the shield but might be embroidered on the clothing of servants or displayed as a banner or pennon. A pennon – a small triangular flag carried on a lance – bore a simplified version of the knight's coat of arms. A larger, typically square or rectangular flag was known as a banner. Both banners and pennons were used by the great nobility and by bannerets, senior knights who led troops in battle.

Women also displayed their coat of arms where appropriate, and passed them to their husband when they married. In these situations, the husband's arms were modified to include half of the wife's arms 'impaled' on the left, or sinister, side of their shield with half of their own on the right (dexter) side. Marriages between powerful families sometimes resulted in a multiply merged crest, which could become extremely complex over time.

Heraldry lost its significance for battlefield recognition once the age of heroic leadership ended, but the concept continued to have meaning in other contexts. elsewhere. Today, heraldic crests are used by nations, cities, families and corporations, with modern corporate logos arguably fulfilling a similar role. Just as a medieval knight might 'build a brand' on the tourney field or in battle, today's symbols serve a similar – though far less violent – purpose. A heraldic crest or company logo communicates identity and often hints at history or heritage to those who see it.

Opposite: Simon de Montfort (1208–65), Earl of Leicester, was a renowned military commander. His prominently displayed arms would inspire confidence in those who fought under him.

INDEX

Illustrations page references are in **bold**.

PICTURE CREDITS

Alamy: 5 (Keith Corrigan), 12 (Prisma Archivo), 14/15 (Peter Barritt), 18/19 (Mauricio Abreu), 27 (The Print Collector), 28 (piemags/POL24), 29 (PjrTravel), 32 (Interfoto), 40/41 (Interfoto), 43 (lunstream), 47 (North Wind Picture Archives), 48/49 (Granger Historical Picture Archive), 50 (De Luan), 53 (Heritage Image Partnership), 60 & 92 (Interfoto), 101 & 114/115 (Album), 117 (Tolo Balaguer), 122 (Peter Lorimer), 130 (The History Collection), 132 (shoricelu), 138 (Smith Archive), 141 (Stephen Dorey), 164/165 (Heritage Image Partnership), 172 (Royal Armouries Museum), 183 (Eddie Linssen) 185 (Granger Historical Picture Archive), 189 (Glasshouse Images), 200 (Dorling Kindersley), 210/211 (Gallery of Art), 213 (Chronicle), 214 (Florilegius), 216 (Universal Images Group)

Art Institute of Chicago: 160/161, 177 far left

Cleveland Museum of Art: 66, 88, 112

Dreamstime: 108/109 (Jorisvo)

Getty Images: 6 (Luisa Vallon Fumi), 10 (Universal History Archive), 45 (Bettmann), 54 (Print Collector), 55 (Photo Josse/Leemage), 56 (Fototeca Storica Nazionale), 59 (Heritage Images), 74/75 (Print Collector), 76 & 80 (Sepia Times), 82 (Photo Josse/Leemage), 118 (Design Pics Editorial), 129 (Heritage Images), 182 & 194/195 (Heritage Images), 198/199 (Print Collector), 201 (Hulton Archive), 217 & 218 (Culture Club), 219 (Photo 12), 221 (Universal History Archive)

Getty Images/De Agostini: 31, 34, 37, 38/39, 42, 98/99, 116, 136/137, 151

Metropolitan Museum of Art, New York: 16, 17, 20/21, 24, 25 ,64, 72, 73, 77, 78, 79, 83, 85, 86, 89, 90, 91, 95, 96, 103, 105, 111, 120/121, 125, 126, 133, 134, 139, 143-150, 154/155, 156, 157, 159 both, 162, 163, 167, 168/169, 176, 177 left & both right, 179, 186/187, 190, 197, 202 both, 203, 207 both, 212

Public Domain: 62/63, 110, 170/171, 174/175

Rijksmuseum, Amsterdam: 208

Walters Art Museum, Baltimore: 22

Yale University Art Gallery: 33

All black-and-white line artworks produced by JB Illustrations for Amber Books.